Grounds for Belief

*The place brought them together;
the discussion changed them forever.*

Ed Dickerson

Pacific Press® Publishing Association
Nampa, Idaho
Oshawa, Ontario, Canada
www.pacificpress.com

Cover design by Gerald Lee Monks
Cover photo iStockphoto.com
Inside design by Steve Lanto

Scripture quotations marked NIV are from the HOLY BIBLE, NEW INTERNA-
TIONAL VERSION, copyright © 1973, 1978, 1984 by the International Bible
Society. Used by permission of Zondervan Bible Publishers.
Scripture quotations marked CEV are from the Contemporary English Version,
copyright © 1991, 1995 by the American Bible Society. Used by permission.
Scripture quotations marked NKJV are from the Holy Bible, New King James
Version, copyright © 1979, 1980, 1982 by Thomas Nelson, Inc. Used by permission.
Scripture quotations marked *The Message* are copyright © 1993 by Eugene H.
Peterson. Used by permission of NavPress Publishing Group.

Library of Congress Cataloging-in-Publication Data

Dickerson, Ed (Edgar Dean), 1950-
Grounds for Belief : the place brought them together, the discussion changed
them forever / Ed Dickerson
p. cm.
ISBN 13: 978-0-8163-2184-1
ISBN 10: 0-8163-2184-1
1. Young adults—Religious life. 2. Christian life—Seventh-Day Adventist
authors. I. Title.

BV4529.2.D53 2007
277.3'0830842—dc22
2006053294

Additional copies of this book are available by calling toll-free 1-800-765-6955 or
by visiting http://www.adventistbookcenter.com.

07 08 09 10 11 • 5 4 3 2 1

Dedicated to

Melvin Rosen.
A mentor in the truest sense,
you saw potential where
others only saw problems.

Acknowledgments

Many individuals played significant roles in bringing this book to the public. Without the continuing encouragement and advocacy of Dr. Jon Paulien of Andrews University and David Marshall of Stanborough Press, this book would not have been written or published. Lee Gallaher, editor of LIFE.info, who gave me the opportunity to write for his wonderful pioneering magazine for a postmodern audience, also read the entire manuscript and gave me much valuable feedback. Tim Lale, my editor at Pacific Press®and Marvin Moore, editor of *Signs of the Times*®, saw promise in my first poor article manuscript. And then there are my children: Ben and Erica Dickerson (the model for the Erica in the book but *not* the same person); Shoshannah and husband, Jonathan Guerrero; Elise and her husband, Jonathan Healzer (Erica and Shoshannah especially championed the real Grounds for Belief café); and all the members of the HomePage, our church plant for the twenty-first century, who supported that ministry. Finally, my life's companion, one of the most courageous and beautiful people I have ever been privileged to know, my wife, Mavis, took on many additional burdens so this book could be written.

Contents

Intro:
God vs. Religion

• • • • •

I don't care much for preachers," David said. As a favor for a church member, I met the newly discharged marine at the airport. Because David had heard me described as a "lay pastor," the twenty-something young man wanted to avoid any misunderstandings—or spontaneous sermons, no doubt.

"I feel the same way," I said. My comment didn't register with him, and he continued. "No, this 'spirituality' stuff is all right, as far as it goes, but I don't really believe in all the stuff I hear about in church."

"There are a lot of things I don't buy either."

That remark stopped him. He ran a hand through his short military haircut and looked at me, slightly puzzled. "But I thought you were into church and things like that? They said you speak at churches and write articles for religious magazines and all—"

"I'm very serious about God," I said, "but 'God' and 'religion' don't always have a lot to do with each other." I knew a little of David's history. He had grown up in a Christian home, attending church school and boarding academy. Not long after 9/11, he enlisted in the Marines and served in Afghanistan and Iraq. Having met a Christian young woman, he wanted to settle down and get married.

His parents had not only condemned him for joining the Marines, but they now questioned his character, his suitability for marriage, his choice of a mate—nearly everything about him. When he attended his hometown church immediately after returning from the service, he heard a sermon condemning a young single mother sitting not far from him. He didn't like it.

When David thought about himself, he thought all those authority figures agreed—that God disapproved of him. Their unanimous verdict: Spiritually, he was hopeless.

Renee, his fiancée, disagreed. She wanted my opinion. She thought I might be able to help him. "Just talk to him a little, please?" He was scheduled on a flight that arrived in the middle of the workday, and she asked me to pick him up. That's how we ended up in my car at the airport.

"If there is a God—" I started.

"Oh, there's a God all right. Once the bullets started flying, everyone wanted God on their side," David said. "But they didn't waste any time with 'thee's' and 'thou's.' "

"Exactly," I said, "and that's the difference between God and religion." I had his attention now. "Most who believe in God, believe He is the Creator and Ruler of the universe, a personal being. Your buddies asked Him for help." David nodded. "*Religion* describes all the ways we talk about God, and try to reach God—the 'thee's' and 'thou's.' "

"I think I see what you're saying. God is 'who,' and religion is 'how.' "

"More or less," I agreed. "The problem comes when we mistake the 'how' for the 'who.' When we start to place more importance on religion, to worship the 'how' instead of 'who,' the real God . . ." I paused, watching this sink in. "And God wants us to be real with Him too."

"What are you saying?"

"I'm saying that lots of people are angry with God—I am sometimes—and it's OK to tell God you're angry with Him. In fact, He'd far rather you honestly admitted your anger than pretend otherwise."

"Are you sure you're a pastor?" David asked. "Seems like most pastors only care about the 'how'—about the 'thee's' and 'thou's.' "

I grinned ruefully. "I'm sorry about that. I know how you feel—oh, here we are!"

I pulled into the parking lot of the apartment complex where he would be staying.

Renee met us. David got out of the car and, after a quick embrace with Renee, retrieved his duffel and one small suitcase. After thanking me for picking him up, he leaned in the car window and said, "Renee mentioned something about a coffee shop?"

"Of course. Our church offers it on Wednesday nights. It's called Grounds for Belief. Come on over and see," I said. "We hang out. Talk. Enjoy snacks. Sometimes we have some entertainment. Games."

"Do you talk about stuff like we did today?" he asked.

"If people want to, sure. It's up to you."

"We just might come," he said.

. ☕ .

Everyone's welcome at our café. Read along and the pages that follow will reveal the type of thing that goes on at Grounds for Belief. The cast of characters changes. Some are pretty much regulars, some come and go. A few come once and never return. We talk about everything there— sports, books and movies, *Friends, The Simpsons*, evolution and creation, *Star Trek* and *Star Wars*, the occult, and toxic religion. Grounds for Belief is a place where we have fun, meet people, learn about life and love, about friendship, trust, and living well.

Most of the conversations in this book represent actual discussions I've had, though sometimes I change details and edit to protect privacy and to make an easier read. A few of the conversations actually took place at other locations, but I've placed them at Grounds for Belief for simplicity's sake.

These discussions don't proceed according to anyone's predetermined schedule, nor do they match some artificial syllabus or series of "steps." But they do have a logic of their own. That's because while some people get stuck on the same question, asking it over and over, most real seekers find answers—which lead to new questions.

No one "steers" or "drives" the discussions. That would be rude. Still, they tend to move toward a common destination. Just as there are cross-currents and eddies in a mighty river while the river as a whole moves toward the sea, so there are differences among spiritual seekers, but as a group they move toward their goals.

What goals? The same goals we all have. *To find answers to the great questions of existence. To make the most of the time we are given.* If that appeals to you, come along and listen in.

Einstein's Question

• • • • •

The only question that really matters is, "Is the universe friendly?"
—Albert Einstein

I don't know if I should be here," David said.

I had the pistol in my hand, so I motioned for him to sit down, which he did without comment. "Mrs. White did it," I said, looking around the table, "with the Pistol, in the Conservatory."

"It's called the revolver," Erica said.

"OK," I relented, "the revolver." I took the envelope from the center and looked inside. Without saying any more, I laid the cards face up: Mrs. White, the Pistol, and the Conservatory.

"That's it," Erica said, "I'm not playing Clue with you anymore." A general noise of agreement rose up as people turned in their cards. "Winner puts the game away," she said. The other players rose and went their various ways.

"Never did trust Mrs. White," David said, and I grinned.

"Is that why you wonder if you should be here?" I asked.

"No. I don't know . . ." He hesitated. Renee, who had been at the counter getting something to drink, walked up and put her hand on his shoulder. David looked up at her, and she nodded. "Well, it's just that people here seem to have all the answers." He shook his head, looking somewhere in the distance. "It's not that simple for me."

11

"It's not that simple for anyone, David," I said. He looked at me quizzically. "I don't have all the answers. Far from it."

"And other people's answers—my parents, for example—their answers don't work for me."

"I agree. We all have to find our own answers. But that's not the hardest part," I said.

"What's the hardest part?" David asked.

"Finding the right question."

"And what question would that be?"

"For you?" I asked, and he nodded once. "I don't know. But I would start with Einstein's question."

"Einstein? I thought he was, like, a genius," David said. "What question could he have?"

"Well, Einstein said, 'The only question that really matters is, "Is the universe friendly?" ' "

"Is it?" David asked.

"W-e-l-l . . . Mind if I tell you a story?" I asked. David agreed, so I began.

· ☕ ·

Have you noticed how the plastic that packaged foods like potato chips come in keeps getting thinner and thinner and at the same time tougher and tougher? I used to be able to open a bag of potato chips with my hands, with a minimum of grunting and grimacing. No more. Maybe advancing age has weakened me, but these days the plastic barely stretches, no matter the amount of wrestling, clenching of muscles, and grunting.

It seemed to me that I should be able to find a more dignified, more elegant means to open a bag of chips. Of course, any time we try something new, there's a chance we'll make a mistake and end up looking foolish.

George Bernard Shaw—he was an author and playwright—commented on this likelihood. "A man learns to skate," he said, "by staggering about making a fool of himself; indeed, he progresses in all things by making a fool of himself."

While what he said is true, there are ways of saying it that make the process easier to face. We do learn through trial and error, but we don't have to make error such a trial.

Since learning requires that I make mistakes and sometimes appear inept, I've come up with a more positive way of looking at it. I didn't invent this saying, but I've found it makes dealing with mistakes easier: "There are no failed experiments, only new data."

In fact, experiments that appear to go very badly often yield the greatest discoveries. For example, Sir Arthur Fleming had a bacterial specimen spoil and go moldy. Instead of discarding the contaminated specimen as a worthless, failed experiment, he examined the "new data." That failed experiment yielded penicillin, the first antibiotic.

· ♨ ·

"You always hear about penicillin in these stories," David said. "I'm beginning to wonder if that's the only really big discovery made by accident."

"Fair enough," I agreed. "Have you heard about the DuPont chemist who forgot to clean up?"

David shook his head, so I continued.

"In the early nineteen thirties a scientist at DuPont—I've forgotten his name—stirred up a mixture of chemicals and left the gooey mess in the beaker overnight, with the glass stirring rod still in it," I said. "The next morning he returned to find the glass rod embedded in a tough, resilient, clear cylinder. His new data became the first acrylic plastic."

Now David bobbed his head from side to side, as though half-convinced.

"Then there is 3M's failed adhesive. The 3M Corporation assigned Spencer Silver to come up with a tough, fast-drying, durable adhesive for a special project in the year nineteen seventy. Silver failed terribly," I said. "The substance he came up with failed every single criterion. Instead of being tough, it was quite gentle; it almost never seemed to dry fully, remaining mildly sticky indefinitely. Durable? Not at all. Surfaces joined with his adhesive could be peeled apart easily. In most companies, that would have qualified the new adhesive as a disaster, quickly discarded and forgotten.

"But 3M takes the 'new data' approach to mistakes. One day several years later, Arthur Fry, *another* 3M scientist, who sang in a church choir, needed some way to mark the hymns for a given day without defacing the delicate pages. He stumbled across Silver's 'failed' adhesive. Fry put it on bright yellow scraps of paper, which he could then attach to the hymnal pages he needed to mark, and remove them later without damaging the fragile paper."

"Is that really how 3M came up with Post-it notes?" asked Renee. "They must have made the company millions of dollars."

"Billions, or so they say," I said.

"Well, OK, what about the plastic bag? The chips?" David prompted me.

"Right. Sorry, sometimes I get sidetracked. Well, here's what happened with the bag of chips," I continued.

"Our family had gone to the park for a picnic, fortified with all the necessary supplies. When they left me alone at the car with the chips, I saw the opportunity to attempt a more dignified, more elegant means of opening the bag," I said.

"Why do I have a bad feeling about this?" Renee asked.

I gave her an annoyed look and continued. "See, the idea came to me one day looking at a bag of chips. The bags are filled to the top at the factory, but time and agitation settles the contents so that, by the time we get them, the bag appears to be almost half filled with air."

"I know what you mean," said David. "Annoying."

"Well, it was the bulge made by that air that gave me the idea," I said. "I figured that if I could compress the air rapidly enough, that would neatly force open a seam in the bag and solve the problem of the infinitely durable plastic at one stroke. So to speak.

"So, on this beautiful spring afternoon, the opportunity for my great experiment finally came," I confided, leaning forward. "I tossed the bag lightly upward in order to catch it in midair as I brought my open hands together in a powerful clapping motion." I accompanied this description with appropriate hand motions. "The first time I failed to clap hard enough, and the bag simply stuck between my hands. Wait, I'm not done yet," I said. For some reason Renee had begun laughing silently. I'm not certain at what. "The second time I caught it just perfectly, and the compressed air opened a seam with a loud report like a gunshot.

"At this point the new data intruded. Only at that moment did it occur to me that the bag had two seams—one on the top and one on the bottom. Ordinarily that would yield an even chance of opening the desired seam, right?" I asked.

David nodded, going along. "Seems reasonable," he said.

"Well, that's when the second bit of new data intruded," I said. Renee was laughing out loud by now, and David's mouth kept twitching. "Gravity assures that the chips always settle to the bottom of the bag, leaving the air space at the top."

"So when you compressed the air in the top of the bag," David said, his voice slowly disintegrating, "the air propelled the chips," and he lost it.

Nodding grimly, I finished his thought. "That's right. In the opposite direction. Straight down. So there I stood, directly behind the trunk of my car, holding the empty bag, a pile of chips at my feet. The explosive sound assured that every person within earshot turned to witness my embarrassment. My son, then a teenager, grinned and said, 'Wow, Dad, new data.' "

"So, what does all that have to do with whether the universe is friendly?" David asked.

"Well, you know, it takes human beings longer to mature than any other animal. That's not because our bodies are the biggest, the fastest, or the strongest." I shook my head. "No, it takes more than twenty years to get all the circuits in our brains hooked up right. God, evolution, fate—whatever designed us—arranged it so that most of that learning comes through trial and error.

"And since most of us learn and grow rather than die, either most errors must be nonfatal, or we possess some warning system to protect us from the really dangerous mistakes. Whichever way that works, to me it says that the universe must be friendly. Otherwise we'd all be dead," I said.

"So God, or whatever, isn't just waiting to pounce on us? To catch us doing something wrong so He can punish us?" David asked. "Is that what you're saying?"

"Well, if God struck down everyone who was angry at Him or questioned the way He's running the universe, well, it seems to me there wouldn't be many people left. But that's my answer. What matters is, what do you think?" I wanted to ask him more, but Rose, who runs Grounds for Belief, had started closing up, and we all got up and left. Whatever David's answer might be, I'd have to wait at least a week to find out.

All Others Pay Cash

David told me about the chips," Jim said, grinning.

David had brought Jim to the café, introducing him as "My best friend from the Marines."

"And you came anyway?" I said, returning his grin.

"It was a near thing," he replied, bobbing his head up and down as he sat leaning forward, clasping and unclasping his hands. "Anyone who would admit that," he shook his head, "well, I don't know . . ." He looked away and his voice trailed off. Then he brightened, looked up again, then quickly looked down. "Dave said it would be OK to ask . . ."

It was an ordinary night at Grounds for Belief. In the corner, four young women frowned in silence, examining a half-filled Scrabble board as if parsing the Dead Sea Scrolls. Another table featured a lively discussion of *Friends* reruns. And two tables over from us, a raucous game of Uno erupted in gales of laughter, as Lucas Enriquez explained his victorious strategy while the rest booed.

Under the cover of all that racket, David spoke softly to me. "Jim's had a couple of tough years," David said. "Deployed to the Middle East twice. The second time, his wife left him." David frowned. "She just walked away. Left a note for him when he got back."

"Wow! That's tough! Sorry, Jim," I said.

Jim just shrugged. "The thing is . . ." He hesitated. "Look, I don't even think I should say this, but—" He spread his hands. "I'd like to find someone," Jim said, almost blushing, "but I just don't trust anyone anymore."

"Anyone?" I asked.

"Well, only David. But we've been through combat together." He stopped fidgeting and looked at the floor. "Look, I shouldn't have said it. Just pretend—"

"Everyone has problems with trust, Jim. Everyone," I said.

A spark of interest lighted his eyes but quickly faded. "I-I don't know," he said. "Not like me."

"In God We Trust. All others pay cash—is that it?" I asked.

He chuckled. "Yeah," he said. "Like that."

"Did you ever think about how much trust it takes to accept cold, hard cash?" I asked.

"Trust?" he said, clearly puzzled.

"Let me tell you. . . ."

· ☕ ·

Years ago I saw that sign for the first time: "In God We Trust, All Others Pay Cash." I've seen it many times since. But I've thought a lot about that sign. No doubt the merchant who displays that sign thinks himself quite the hard-headed skeptic. In fact, the opposite is true.

Take a look at this cash idea. In exchange for something real, our skeptical shopkeeper insists on—pieces of paper? Bits of metal? But why? I mean, you can't eat a fifty-dollar bill. Well, I suppose you could, but I don't think anyone seeks currency for its nutritional value.

You can burn paper money, but it doesn't provide much heat, and coins don't burn well at all. Bills are too small to keep the rain off your head.

So, we have this strange thing we call cash. By itself it isn't anything *real*, yet you can readily exchange it for real things. So, what gives cash its cachet?

David groaned. Jim just shook his head and said, "David warned me."

I gave him an innocent look that said, "What can I do?"

"OK, OK, you've got me," Jim said. "What gives cash its value?"

"Trust, of course," I said.

"Trust? You're not serious."

"As serious as can be," and I continued.

Consider the German mark—that was their "dollar bill" until they adopted the euro. At the end of World War I, a loaf of bread in war-torn Germany cost just a little more than half a mark. Three years later the price of that same loaf of bread jumped to 163 marks. And that price rise came despite bumper crops of wheat and decreased demand. During peacetime, you have more workers to produce food and fewer soldiers to feed. But that's not the worst. One year later, the price of a single loaf of bread soared to 201,000,000 marks.

"Wait a minute. Wait just a minute," Jim said. "How do you remember stuff like that?"

"Have you seen *Monk*, the detective show?" I asked.

"Yeah, sure."

"Well, it's a gift—and a curse," I said, echoing the obsessive-compulsive Monk's description of his abilities.

Jim rolled his eyes. "All right then. I'll bite. Why *did* the price of bread in Germany go up so fast?"

"Because the German people no longer trusted the government that issued the money. So, they didn't trust the money either," I explained. "And every time you accept money, whether here or in a foreign country, you're trusting that, in turn, you will be able to exchange that money for something you want. It's all about trust. But not just when it comes to money.

"Every day we exchange, build, and lose trust in a myriad ways," I continued. "As we walk down the street, we trust drivers not to swerve and hit us; we trust others waiting in line not to pull out knives and start attacking; we trust restaurant workers not to contaminate or poison our food. People rarely do such things, but they could. Like it or not, we trust strangers with our lives and safety every day. Scary, isn't it?"

"I never thought of it that way," Jim said.

"Of course not. You'd go crazy if you did," I said. "I mean, really crazy. Thinking about all the things that could happen makes you paranoid—you know, thinking people are out to get you. Paranoid people act one of two ways." I paused. Jim, wide-eyed, nodded for me to go on. So, I did. . . .

· 🍵 ·

In one episode of *Monk* we met Monk's brother, Ambrose, who hadn't left his house for thirty years. That's one way to deal with failure to trust. You simply retreat from the world, giving people few chances to hurt you. But even that extreme behavior doesn't eliminate the need for trust. *Someone* has to deliver the groceries, provide the water and power, and make repairs.

Other paranoid people become predators. Their motto is "Do unto others before they do unto you." They hurt and exploit others.

So, there we have it. We can't live without trust. And if we try to minimize our need for trust, we either become predators or we become paralyzed.

· 🍵 ·

"So, what do I do?" Jim asked. "I don't want to become like either one of those, but I feel it happening, feel myself shrinking down and in. But trusting frightens me."

"I hear you, Jim. Trust is frightening for everyone. All the more so when we've been hurt by someone we cared deeply for." I sighed. "I wish I had an easy answer, but I don't."

"I was afraid you'd say that," Jim said.

"I don't have an easy answer, but I do have an answer, one that works for me."

Jim clasped his hands and then opened them like a book. He took a deep breath, turned his head toward me, and nodded once.

The first thing you have to realize is that trust equals risk. To say "I trust you with my garbage" means nothing at all. I don't care what happens to garbage. Since there's no risk, there's no real trust either. If I trust you with a fifty-dollar bill, that's a fifty-dollar risk. Trusting you with my friendship or my love represents an even greater risk.

Second, trust has to be given before it can be earned. That's what makes it so tricky. Over time, my behavior may justify your trust, but you'll never know until you actually take a risk. Think about it. Suppose you give me a fifty-dollar bill for safe keeping. If you call me up every day to see if it's still safe, you're not trusting me. Only if you trust me first can I then earn your trust by returning it when you request it. But, of course, you then run the risk that I might not return it. That's what trust means.

As if it weren't complicated enough, no one is completely trustworthy. Not you. Not me. We all make mistakes. Your fifty-dollar bill might fall out of my pocket when I pull my mobile phone out, or it might get lost in the laundry. We do not know the future. Someone might rob me and take your fifty-dollar bill in the process. Or a fire might break out and consume it. Sometimes our resolve weakens; we can't even trust ourselves. With an unexpected opportunity to go to a concert, I might use your fifty-dollar bill, intending to pay you back, but not have it when you ask for it. I'm not proud of these things; I'm just trying to be realistic.

• ☕ •

"You're not making it any easier," Jim said. "How am I supposed to learn to trust?"

"Well, here's what I've learned," I said. "Be willing to trust first. Don't be suspicious all the time. But be wise about it. A Russian proverb says, 'Trust, but verify.' Remember that trustworthy people are people who trust. Every healthy relationship has to run both ways. So, be cautious when the other person wants to trust you much more or much less than you are ready to trust them. In that light, don't jump in the deep end. Don't trust a new acquaintance with the keys to your car, for example. Start small, increase trust gradually, and be patient. Let trust mature and grow."

"Is that it?" Jim asked.

"Not quite. We have to learn to forgive," I said. "Here's where 'Forgive us as we forgive others' comes into play. Remember, no one is perfectly safe, not even you. I've had to forgive my wife and my best friends, and they have had to forgive me, over and over. This doesn't weaken these relationships. On the contrary, when friends ask for and receive forgiveness, broken relationships knit like broken bones, becoming stronger than before."

"Is that everything?" Jim asked.

"Just a little more. Finally, learn to pardon small faults. 'Do unto others as you would have others do to you.' Everyone has idiosyncrasies that annoy others. We can either learn to overlook these small faults, or be lonely."

"I don't know," Jim said. "That sounds pretty difficult."

I grimaced. "You've got me there," I agreed. "It *is* difficult. But it's more difficult trying to live without trust. It's like that 'cold, hard, cash,'" I said.

Jim shook his head, "I don't follow you."

"Trust is the currency of all our relationships. We can hoard trust, like misers, only to see it dwindle. Or like careful investors, we can put it at risk. The losses yield knowledge to help us invest more wisely next time. The successes can yield dividends as long as we live."

"I never thought of it that way," Jim said. "I suppose you're right. Still, it's frightening to me."

"Absolutely," I said. "It won't be easy, but it will be worth it. Trust me." And we both grinned.

Stuck in Second Gear

• • • •

Think where man's glory most begins and ends,
And say my glory was I had such friends.
—W. B. Yeats

A soft rain fell, muting the sounds of early evening traffic as the cars kept pace with their mirrored reflections on the slick streets. Inside Grounds for Belief a few subdued patrons were scattered among the small tables. Rose had booked a singer for that night, a young woman named Caroline who strummed her guitar and sang soft sad songs. Other than that, the only sounds were the rings of commerce issuing from the cash register.

A slow night at the café. But I didn't mind, because I had spotted a couple of Rose's renowned raspberry turnovers in the pastry case on the counter. As soon as Caroline finished her set and the scattered applause faded, I got up and secured a cup of hot chocolate and one of the raspberry turnovers. Back at the table, I bit into the turnover and held the morsel on my tongue. Eyes closed, I meditated on the richness of life.

"Excuse me." A female voice startled me out of my reverie. I opened my eyes to see the singer, Caroline, her guitar in a case at her feet, head down, peering into my eyes. I swallowed the bite of turnover and grabbed for a napkin, suddenly aware of the bits of glazing and pastry crust around my mouth. "I'm Caroline," she said, covering her mouth to hold a giggle.

22

"Hi," I said, swiping at my mouth. "Uh, hi," I said again, feeling increasingly foolish.

"I was the one singing," she said with a grin, unable to hide her amusement.

"Right, uh . . . uh . . ." For some reason, I couldn't think of anything to say.

"Did you like it?"

"I always like Rose's raspberry turnovers," I said, but she started giggling again. "Your singing! Yes! Please, I'm so embarrassed." I swallowed once, gathered myself. "Yes. You have a lovely voice."

Her expression turned a bit skeptical, but she still blushed slightly. "Thank you." She sat down in a chair, placed her hands in her lap, licked her lips, and looked around the room before she addressed me again. "Would you mind if I asked you a question?"

"Sure. I can answer all your questions, because I can say, 'I don't know,' " I said, recovering.

She looked at her hands in her lap, gave a shy smile. "Rose said . . . sometimes . . ."

I ducked my head to look directly in her eyes, "It's OK. I only bite raspberry turnovers." She looked up and smiled again, and I continued, "All right, all right. I've been known to have a brownie now and then. Is that what Rose has been telling you?"

She paused, considered for a moment, and then said, "She says you help people . . . with their problems . . . sometimes."

"I do what I can. I don't have any magic answers, but I can listen, if that's what you need."

She nodded and began to talk.

· ☕ ·

At twenty-three years of age, Caroline was bright and attractive. She had a job in information technology that paid well enough for her to drive a nice car and live in a comfortable apartment. She had everything she needed, except friends. In fact, she said that except for George, her cat, she didn't have anyone to talk to. That was her problem. Like many others her age, she struggled with loneliness. She longed for friends but didn't know how to build friendships.

"Can you help me?" she asked. "Or do you just think I'm being silly?"

"Silly? Oh no. Far from it," I said. "We may have to travel much of our life's journey by ourselves, but we all need good friends. We need people who care about us, who question us, keep us on our toes. More than a hundred fifty years ago, a man named Henry David Thoreau concluded that most of us live in quiet desperation."

Caroline had been listening carefully. Now I saw tears welling in her eyes. I handed her a clean napkin and said, "You're not alone. Every day, I meet more bewildered people who ask, 'How can I make friends?' So I've given it a lot of thought and come up with some ideas that seem to work. Do you have something to write on?"

She wiped her tears and reached into the purse at her feet. With pen and paper in hand, she said, "Please?"

So, here's what I told her. . . .

Start with you, with your own interests. Friendships revolve around a common enthusiasm. Rather than waiting, frustrated, for friends to materialize, spend time developing your own potential for friendship.

You and I, and every one of us are unique—unrepeatable and incomparable. The more we explore and develop this uniqueness, the more interesting we become to others. Also, the more we understand about ourselves, the more we have to share in a friendship. The more uniqueness we bring to the surface, the more it draws the interest of others.

"I don't feel unique," Caroline said. "What do I have to offer?"

"More than you can imagine. For example, you like to play the guitar, to sing."

"Well, sure, but . . ." She sat, stunned.

"That's part of your uniqueness. Look for others who like music. Some of them might make good friends. But that's just one thing," I said. "Are you interested in antiques? Join a club, go to an antiques fair, find a dealer. Enjoy reading a good book? Many libraries have reading discussion groups. People who like to do the things you enjoy are excellent candidates for friendship."

"That sounds OK," Caroline said. "But I'm lonely now."

. ☕ .

I know you want friends now and want to bypass this step, but friendships work best when they're balanced. Each friend must bring something to the common table, must contribute to the relationship. If you bring only your need for friends to the relationship, you're likely to attract others who bring only a need for friends. All needs and no interests make for a pretty poor friendship.

And you can do much better. You have much to offer others. You only need to take a little time to discover it. As you explore your uniqueness, you will be more contented and less dependent on others for happiness. It's a paradox, but the less we crave friendship, the more likely we are to find it.

Next, realize that friends are like investments. Financial advisors recommend that investors diversify their portfolios—make many small investments of different types—to limit risk. In the same way, it's smarter to invest in many casual friendships rather than put everything into just one or two relationships.

. ☕ .

"I learned that the hard way," Caroline said.

"Want to talk about it?"

"Not really. Just that more than once, I've become deeply involved with one friend, only to have that friend disappoint me. Listening to you," she said, "I realize my mistake. I had so much energy invested in just one or two people and no other friends to support me. So, when that one person disappointed me, I really felt depressed."

"That's the advantage of building many more casual friendships. Like anything else, the more experience you get in building relationships, the better you become at it. Making many casual friends—many small investments—allows you to acquire that experience at low emotional cost. On the other hand, starting one or two relationships and investing deeply right away makes you vulnerable to the devastating experiences you described."

"So, you're saying it's better to have many good friends to begin with, rather than one or two deep ones," Caroline asked.

"That's right. And don't worry," I said, watching for her reaction, "deep relationships, perhaps even love, will grow naturally with time."

She looked up with a trace of a smile. "How do I know if it's safe to invest more in a relationship?"

"Remember what your mother told you about crossing the street?"

"You mean, 'Look both ways'?" Caroline asked.

"Exactly. Healthy relationships go both ways. So, keep watching to see that the relationship remains balanced, reciprocal."

"Could you explain that?"

"Of course . . ."

· ☕ ·

When you get together, does your friend continually talk about himself or herself, not letting you have equal time? Does the other person make dogmatic statements, but if you disagree he/she gets abusive? Does the other person unload his/her feelings of disappointment and anger but never have time to hear your feelings? Does your friend speak of your failings but doesn't talk about theirs? Of course, it might happen in any relationship once in a while, but if it continues over time, you may have trouble.

Any time you discover that a relationship has become seriously one-sided, you need to back off a little to restore balance. If the relationship cannot be balanced, then you have two choices. Either end the relationship or reduce your investment to a level where you can tolerate the emotional loss.

· ☕ ·

"How do I know how much to 'back off'?" Caroline asked.

"Ah yes. A friend of mine, Dr. Bill Underwood, taught me about the seven levels of friendship. That really helps me in my own relationships. I don't have them with me, but I'll be glad to send them to you in an e-mail."

"I'd like that," Caroline said. (To see what I sent her, look at Table 1.) "But I have another question." I nodded assent, so she asked. "What if I can't get a friendship balanced? Do I have to lose a friend?"

You can't keep a relationship healthy unless you're determined to end it if it becomes unhealthy. When continuing the relationship becomes more important than keeping it balanced, it grows increasingly parasitic, manipulative, and destructive.

You're far better off enjoying a healthy relationship at level two or three (see Table 1) than taking that relationship to level five or six, only to have it grow manipulative or abusive. Not everyone is ready for a deep relationship. But that's OK. You may know someone who chatters on pleasantly about things you care about. It does no harm to enjoy that person's company so long as you don't risk more than that particular friendship can sustain. I've had golfing companions who had nothing more than level three to contribute to the relationship. We don't confide our deep concerns to each other, but that doesn't prevent us from sharing a pleasant time together. Besides, after a period of soul-searching, such companions can bring welcome relief. No matter how much we love to dive deep, everyone has to come up for air sometimes.

On the other hand, if you discover that you're spending all your time and emotional energy on relationships unlikely to progress beyond level two or three, it might be wise to go back and explore your own uniqueness again. You may possess as yet undiscovered depths.

Diversifying your emotional investments in many friends builds a reservoir of emotional strength. You can more readily sustain any single loss, or even a series of losses. This reservoir allows you to put more at risk, to develop other deeper relationships safely.

· ☕ ·

We both sat quietly for a bit. "Anything else I need to know?" Caroline inquired.

"Be patient," I replied. "Good friendships, like the sweetest fruit, ripen slowly. Rushing a relationship can distort and cripple it, sometimes permanently. If you're feeling impatient, go back to the beginning. Start more first-level friendships; diversify while you wait for growth in existing relationships. It's always worthwhile, makes you a better friend, and provides the foundation for greater growth."

"Excuse me," said a young man with a dense mop of curly brown hair. "Is that your guitar?" He looked at me.

"Actually, it belongs to this young woman," I said, inclining my head toward Caroline.

"Really?" he said. "Is that a Gibson? 'Cause it looks a lot like one I've been wanting to get." Caroline indicated that it was, indeed, a Gibson, and he asked, "Would you mind if I played it a little?"

After the first ten minutes they spent talking guitars and trading riffs, I decided to excuse myself and take the rest of my raspberry turnover to another table. They barely looked up as I left.

Table 1 The Seven Levels of Friendship

Level	Description	Examples
1	Surface	Weather, time of day, general information: The kind of thing you might say to someone in a queue at the grocery store or the airport.
2	Facts and reports	More specific information, including personal but not private information such as name, marital status, occupation, time of next bus, etc.
3	Opinions and judgments	What you think about a whole range of things from current events, sports, your favorite TV show—to religion, politics, and morality
4	Feelings	Your personal emotional status and reaction to various situations
5	Vulnerability	Admitting your faults to another
6	Intimacy	They can tell you about faults you do not see in yourself.
7	Complete	Total openness, total trust

Source: Dr. William H. Underwood. Used by permission. All rights reserved.

You're Born, Life's a Pain, and Then?

* * * *

There he is!" a voice said, and a smattering of applause greeted me as I
walked into the café the next Wednesday night. "Looks OK to me,"
said another.

Puzzled, I said, "I'll have to come late more often."

From a table near the far wall, David said, "Rose was worried."

I looked toward the kitchen and saw Rose bustling about, and she
appeared not to hear. I waved hello to Holly, Rose's pregnant niece, a
sweet, sad girl who helped her in the kitchen most evenings.

"There was an accident on the interstate, just north of my exit. Backed
up traffic and made me late," I said. When Rose still gave no notice, I
walked over to David's table, in response to his welcoming gesture. Renee
smiled a greeting.

"Rose heard about the accident on the radio," David said, keeping his
voice low. "Two people were killed." He paused, tilting his head toward
the kitchen. "She was afraid maybe you were one of them."

"Well, like Mark Twain said, 'Rumors of my demise are somewhat
exaggerated.' " I smiled, looking toward the kitchen. But Rose still paid
no notice. Holly shrugged.

"What's with her?" Renee asked. "She was so worried, but now she
acts as if it never happened."

"She's lost a lot of people close to her. Death is a touchy subject with
her," I said, also keeping my voice down.

"Death's touchy with everyone, isn't it?" David asked. "Funerals and funeral parlors give me the creeps."

"You should see my wife," I said. "We can't go into a museum together if there's a mummy anywhere on the premises."

"Why? How bad could it be?" Renee asked, a little offended for my wife, I thought.

"Well, would you want to be seen in public with someone shivering, screaming, and blubbering incoherently?" I paused. "Well, neither would she," I said.

David groaned, and Renee made a face.

"OK, OK, you've heard it before, but, work with me, will you?"

"Seriously, though," Renee said, "one of my classmates is a Goth, you know? Dresses in black, talks about death all the time. Depressing." She made a face. "Says death is just the next step of life." Another face. "What do you think?"

"Death. Well, we like to ignore it, but it just won't go away. Ernest Hemingway said, 'Every true story ends in death.' " I took a deep breath.

"Fine," said David. "It's a great plot device for novels, films, and TV dramas. But I'd rather not think about it right now, thank you. It's depressing."

"Believe me, I know how you feel. You may have noticed that I try to ignore the topic. If that fails, I try to fend it off with black humor," I said.

"But like my classmate says," Renee said, "we all face it."

"That's true," I said . . .

· ☕ ·

No matter how much we dislike it, no matter what our age, we all live but one breath, one heartbeat from death. We all recognize it's inevitable—"death and taxes" and all that—but we resist the topic in general and flatly refuse to contemplate it personally. I don't like thinking about death in general, and I really hate thinking about my own death.

In ancient times, when life was short and death ever present, people thought a lot about death. Thousands of years ago, a man named Job took on this issue and came up with a saying that really resonates with me. Without the press of telecommunications, cars, computers, and microwave ovens, people took life a little slower back then, so I'll translate and condense Job's ornate language:

Job 14:1, 2, NIV	Ed's Modern Translation
" 'Man, born of woman	*You're born*
is of few days and full of trouble	*Life's a pain*
. . . he does not endure.' "	*Then you die*

. ☕ .

"You're kidding," David said. "That sounds like what my buddies in the Marines used to say."

"That was really written, like, thousands of years ago?" Renee asked. As we talked, conversation at nearby tables stopped and others leaned forward, listening.

"Absolutely," I replied. "Technology may have given us e-mail, the incandescent light, and flush toilets, but when it comes to death, we face the same questions as the builders of the pyramids. So, their answers might be useful to us."

"What answers did they come up with?" David asked. An agreeing murmur arose.

"It's really pretty simple," I explained. "All the people who wondered about death over thousands of years arrived at two basic possibilities: Either death ends everything, or it does not."

"Well, which is it?" Caroline had pulled up a chair.

"How about if I share the various answers they came up with?" I asked. "Then you decide for yourselves." Heads bobbed up and down.

So I began . . .

. ☕ .

All the really old cultures believed in some sort of existence after death. Eastern religions believed that life followed death in a cycle of reincarnation. They viewed life as characterized by pain. They believed that doing bad things in this life condemned them to bad karma, to being reborn with even more suffering in the next life. So, they tried to live blamelessly once and thus escape more life and more pain. They used meditation to minimize pain, avoid evil deeds, and "become one with everything," to achieve Nirvana. A person fortunate enough to die while in a state of Nirvana avoids rebirth, and thus more pain. To summarize the view of Eastern mystics, using our modern paraphrase of Job: *"Life's a pain. You're born. If you fail, you're reborn. Life's a pain. If you fail, you're reborn. Life's a pain . . .* and so on till you get it right. *Then you die."*

Ancient Egyptians, Mayas, Baal worshipers, the Chinese—all believed that death marked not the end of all life, but a transition to another type of life. From the discoveries at King Tut's tomb, the Central American pyramids, and ancient tombs in the Middle East and China, we know that all these religions looked forward to an afterlife very much like this life. Kings and wealthy citizens furnished their tombs with every comfort so they would be adequately prepared to enjoy the next life.

Even the monotheistic religions, the ones that teach there is only one God—Judaism, Christianity, and Islam—all teach that death need not be the end. In every case, these religions speak of an afterlife that resembles our current life: much, much better for the righteous, or much worse. Using our model, we'll express the view of these religions this way: *"You're born, life's a pain, but there's a much better (or much worse) life after you die."*

. ☕ .

"You said there were two notions?" Mark had joined the group.

Nodding, I said, "Right. Either death ends everything, or it does not. Like I said, all the ancient religions said death doesn't end everything."

"But what about the idea that death *does* end everything? That's what science says," Mark said.

. ☕ .

The notion that death ends everything is of relatively recent vintage. Today people take what I call a naturalistic view. For the naturalist, death represents only a stage in "the great circle of life." According to this view, the body decomposes after death, and all of those molecules that made up "you" will nourish plant life, which some animal consumes. Given enough cycles, your molecules will eventually become part of some new human being, who will eventually die and start the cycle again.

Like Eastern mysticism, naturalism believes in reincarnation of sorts. Naturalists aren't reborn personally, but some of their molecules may be part of another living organism someday. Eastern mystics attempt to "become one with everything" voluntarily, through meditation; naturalists do it involuntarily and at a molecular level. Think of this as "Eastern mysticism lite."

Summarizing this view yields the following: *"You're born, life's a pain, you're fertilizer."*

Another and related modern view arises from Darwinism, or evolution. Evolution declares that "successful" organisms, including human beings, live on through the genetic information they leave behind in their offspring. As an individual you don't really matter at all; only the increasingly complex genetic information you leave behind is significant.

. ☕ .

"In some ways this is the most depressing theory of all," I said.

"But why would you say that?" Caroline asked.

"It's really bad news for people who never have children," I said. "Whether they're celibate all their lives, sterile, or homosexual. Since they don't bequeath their genetic information to any future generation, this sidelines them from the great evolutionary journey, and forever maroons their uniqueness to oblivion—like they never existed. As far as evolution's concerned, they're irrelevant."

"That *is* depressing," said David.

"It certainly would be, but in the end—according to the Darwinian view—it doesn't matter all that much, since we're all doomed anyway."

"What do you mean?" This from Renee.

. ☕ .

Evolution says you only exist in the first place because of random accidents. Life, which came about accidentally, will be destroyed without purpose. As everything continues evolving merrily along, eventually the dying sun will explode and vaporize this earth, taking all life with it. Even if life exists elsewhere in the universe, all stars eventually burn out, leaving behind a universe too cold to sustain life. The universe that began with a fiery Big Bang ends with an icy whimper.

That makes life the universe's idea of black humor, and the joke's on us.

We can describe this view as follows: *"You're born by accident. Life is a bad joke, a hiccup in the life of the universe. You die. Eventually everything dies."*

. ☕ .

"So, which one's right?" David asked.

"That's the problem," I said. "We must choose among these alternatives, but we possess no direct means of verifying them."

"So if we can't know with certainty which of these theories about death is true, why bother thinking about it?" David said. "Sounds like a waste of time."

"It would be," I agreed, "except that what we believe about death influences the way we live. If there's no great tomorrow after life's today, then it makes sense to get the most pleasure out of today. On the other hand, if today's evil deeds must be paid for in the endless cycle of reincarnation or eternal hellfire, then we would be wise to live accordingly. If there's a glorious tomorrow called heaven or Paradise to win, we'd be foolish not to take that into account."

"OK," David said. "I see what you're saying. So, how do we choose?"

"You'll have to make up your own mind." I said. "But I can share what influences my own choice."

"Let's have it," David said, accompanied by an agreeing chorus.

"Don't keep us waiting," said Renee.

"All right. Are we agreed that as much as we may enjoy life, no one believes this world to be perfect? We share a sense that, at the deepest level, something has gone wrong?" I asked. Hearing no objection, I went on. . . .

. ☕ .

Whether by design or through natural selection, each of the experiences common to us all—growing up, maturing, falling in love, making love, having children—give us intense pleasure and great joy. All except one. Only death frightens us; it seems out of place. Death offends us, death appalls us, seems an insult to nature. Poet Dylan Thomas expressed this natural sense of outrage: "Do not go gentle in that good night / Rage, rage against the dying of the light."

It seems that if death truly belonged in this world, we should not dread it any more than we dread the transition from childhood to adulthood. It might be unwelcome, like losing our hair or needing spectacles, but we shouldn't regard it with fear and loathing. But we do.

· ☕ ·

"So, what does it all mean?" Renee asked, and once again a confirming murmur arose around the room.

"It leads me to a simple conclusion: Of all life's common experiences, death seems wrong because it *is* wrong; it seems unnatural because it *is* unnatural. We hate saying goodbye because *we were not meant to say goodbye.*"

"And . . ." Renee prompted me.

"And . . . if death *is* out of place, if it *does not* belong here, if it *is* as contrary to nature as we sense it to be, then maybe all the religions are right," I said. "Maybe everything will be set right again. Maybe the tangled web of death will unravel, its stranglehold will be broken once and for all, and those who embrace life will receive it again. Maybe, as an old book says, the day will come when ' "there will be no more death . . . for the old order of things has passed away" ' [Revelation 21:4, NIV]."

"Do you believe that?" David asked. I surveyed the now silent room.

"Yes, I do. Hemingway said, 'Every true story ends in death,' but I believe the truest story of all ends in life."

Renee started to say something, but it was past closing time, and Rose came and began herding us out of the café. I noticed some very pleasant aromas coming from the kitchen, and just as I reached the exit, Rose pressed a small brown paper bag into my hands but said not a word. I looked inside the bag and saw two fresh raspberry turnovers and a small note that said, "Drive carefully."

This Moment

. . . . .

I made the mistake of playing Uno with Lucas Enriquez and Mark MacKenzie. Except for their passion for the card game, Lucas, the musician, and Mark, the accountant, are nothing alike. They're great guys, but they play Uno with the kind of concentration a shark gives to its next meal. Round after round, whichever one played his final card first, it seemed that I always ended up with a handful of cards. Despite my pathetic showing, watching those two go at it kept me entertained. That, and my lame jokes about how badly I was playing, kept everyone laughing. Eventually, we got so noisy that others began gathering around our table.

"More people wanting to witness my humiliation," I said. The evening had progressed to the point where almost anything was funny, and this got a laugh.

"What is it with you?" David said.

"You mean the lame jokes?"

"Well, sort of. Someone told me you lost your desktop computer to lightning last week. Is that true?" David again.

"Oh, that. Yup. I was sitting at the computer when I heard a loud snap. *Then* I heard the thunderclap. Fried the motherboard," I admitted.

"But I also heard that your laptop died three days later."

"Yeah. What can I say?" I asked. "Wasn't a good week for me and computers."

"And you got a traffic ticket?" David said.

"OK. Stop. Now you're even depressing me," I chuckled.

"How can you be like that? Your week really sucked, and here you are laughing like nothing happened. How do you do that?" David asked.

"Well, I won't pretend the week has been all laughs," I admitted. "I've had my ups and downs all right. But what would you expect me to do?"

"I don't know. But if all that happened to me, I'd have a hard time partying and having fun. How do you do it?"

"Hmmm. Well, let me tell you about a couple of people I knew. . . ."

. ☕ .

Eileen died Christmas Day, 2003, a few months short of her ninetieth birthday. A rich, full life, you might say. If only that were so. I rarely saw her happy. For reasons I can only guess, she always looked on the dark side of life. Fears of many kinds haunted her, and sometimes it appeared as if she actively sought reasons to be unhappy.

After her children married and moved away, Eileen called and wrote, telling them how unhappy she was at their absence. Yet, when they visited her, her joy lasted for only about thirty minutes before the dark clouds of her nature rolled in, and she returned to her accustomed misery. On almost any occasion, no matter how intrinsically joyful or festive, she quickly found reason to be afraid or angry or—most often—hurt. Not surprisingly her grandchildren soon found Grandma's presence unwelcome. It took a great deal of parental coaxing, explaining how much Grandma really loved them—eventually, some outright bribery—to convince them to spend time with her.

Nine years before her death, she took offense at a letter her only son sent her and shut him out of her life. Her second husband read the letter and saw nothing objectionable in it, but Eileen refused to discuss it, and no one could change her mind. Not long after that letter, she suffered a series of debilitating strokes, and she lived most of the last decade of her life alone, with only strangers to care for her. It still saddens me to think of all those lost years, now gone beyond recovery.

By contrast, Amos preceded Eileen in death by nearly thirty years. A brain tumor took his vigor, and then his life, before he reached his sixtieth birthday. A life cut short, you might say. Perhaps, but what it lacked in length, he made up for in breadth of spirit.

The sort of fellow who brightened every room he entered, Amos had a smile, a joke, a wink, or a pat on the back for each one he met, according to their tastes. He rarely complained about anything, except in jest. He bore such a strong resemblance to the actor Clark Gable that people stopped him on the street, remarking on the likeness. A master carpenter and cabinet maker, Amos could take ordinary boards and fashion them into objects of useful beauty. He put together a construction crew of skilled but eccentric workers who had refused to work for anyone else. People who barely knew him loved him. Whether at work, or stopping at a market, wherever he went, people smiled. When he died, the lady who ran the fruit market down the street cried.

· ☕ ·

"Did one live during a war or famine or something and the other during times of peace and prosperity?" Renee asked. "Circumstances like that can make a lot of difference."

"Actually, both Eileen and Amos grew up and married during the Depression," I explained. "Then came World War Two and more hardship. Amos worked hard all his life, but he never accumulated wealth. One day I asked him how he managed to stay cheerful almost all the time, given the hard life he had lived. 'Well,' he said, 'life is so full of trials and disappointments that you have two choices. You can laugh or you can cry. I enjoy laughing more. Besides, when things are at their worst, they've got nowhere to go but up.' "

"Sounds good," David said. "But I don't believe it. When things get really tough, it's just not that easy."

"I didn't say it was easy," I replied. "But time and again I've witnessed the truth of his statement. Have you ever seen anyone who's suffered a devastating loss, or been stricken by accidents or disease, and yet chose to be happy?"

"It always amazed me how upbeat Christopher Reeve was," Renee said. "Movie star, rich. Then his riding accident, and he was a quadriplegic." This accompanied by general agreement.

"Yet, some people with health, wealth, and privilege are miserable," I added, to more nods and murmurs.

Mark rarely spoke, but now he asked, "So. What makes the difference, do you think?"

"A couple of things," I said.

· ☕ ·

First, happiness is a choice. We can choose to enjoy whatever good comes our way, and hope for more, or we can wallow in misery over what we lack. Possessions, status, education, accomplishment—all those things have little to do with happiness. Circumstances cannot make us happy. Only we can choose to be happy.

Second, none of us knows the future. We can fill that blank canvas with hope or with fear. Nearly half a century before her death, Eileen told her preschool son that she would be dead before his father came home that evening. Eileen let the fear of sickness and death cast a shadow over her life for at least forty years. Then, when debilitating illness struck, she longed to die. She had eighty healthy, active years—eight decades she could have filled with joy and love. But she allowed fear and gloom to isolate her from those who loved her, and she lived in misery instead. Amos lived only fifty-nine years, but he filled fifty-eight of them with happiness and good humor. Even during his last year, bedridden, he smiled often. Eileen lived half again as long as Amos, but not half so well.

Third, we only have today. I've lost friends who died early in life and known others who lived into their tenth decade. Without exception, the happy ones live in the only moment any of us really has—this present one. If we don't learn to enjoy this moment, we will never enjoy any moment. Eileen lived in fear because she spent much of her time worrying about the unknowable future instead of enjoying the present. Amos chose to find the joy in the moment, no matter how small. Fresh-baked bread, the smell of new mown hay, a laugh shared with a friend or a loved one, whatever small joys the present offered.

· ☕ ·

"How do you know so much about these people you keep talking about?" David asked. "I'm beginning to think you just made them up."

"Understandable," I said. "They do seem conveniently opposite, I suppose. But they were very real. Eileen was my mother, and Amos was my father." The room grew very quiet.

"Because of their very different influence on my life, David, I'm tempted to swing from optimism to fear. But both of their lives taught me that a full and happy life has little to do with its length and everything to do with what we choose now. I can let my thoughts be filled with regrets about the past, laments about what I don't have, or fear of the future. But when I do, I spend that time in misery."

"I'm sorry," David said. "I didn't know—"

"It's fine, David," I said. "I understand you wanting to know how real this experience was for me. That's fair."

"As far as my recent misfortunes, well, I'm still here," I said. "I've learned that most of my fears focus on the future, yet I can't live there. The vast majority of those fears never come to pass, but worrying about them wears me out today. In most cases, they concern things that I can do nothing to avoid anyway, so that energy was doubly wasted."

"Yeah. I guess that's right," said David.

"On the other hand, when I fill today with optimism and joy, I build pleasant memories that provide comfort for tomorrow and give me strength to face whatever comes," I said, gathering up the abandoned Uno cards on the table. "Someday death will take me. Until then, he can wait outside. I refuse to let him spoil the party going on today. How about you?" I handed the deck to Lucas, who began shuffling. "Another hand of Uno?"

Naughty, but Not Nice

* * * * *

I've heard a lot about this place," Stan Snyder said, "so I thought I'd come check it out personally. Maybe help you fine-tune your efforts." I tried not to show my annoyance. It seemed to me that Snyder, a senior pastor for one of the largest local churches, and a noted evangelist, couldn't always distinguish between his opinion and what God might be thinking. He had obviously "dressed down" for the occasion, wearing a sweater over his dress shirt and tie, and was looking askance at my sweatshirt and jeans.

"My 'efforts,' as you call them, are to enjoy a quiet evening," I said.

"That's not what I was led to believe," Snyder insisted. "What are you teaching these people?"

"It's not a matter of *me* teaching *these people*," I said. "This is a place where people can have some fun, be with friends, and talk about whatever they want to. Safely." He looked skeptical, so I continued. "Look, I don't know who told you about us, or what they said," I explained, "but there's nothing formal going on here. We hang out, play some games, talk, have fun."

People had begun filtering in, dispersing themselves around the other tables, Snyder examining each one. Several gestured or spoke brief greetings which I returned, but for some reason no one joined us, and the usually animated atmosphere remained subdued. Then Snyder saw Holly, seven months and very pregnant, serving hot chocolate to a

41

patron. Holly's live-in boyfriend had suddenly left when he found out she was expecting. Now she lived with her aunt Rose and worked part time at the café.

"What is that girl doing here?" Snyder asked, a little too loudly for my comfort.

"If you mean Holly, she helps Rose in the kitchen," I said. Unfortunately, I hadn't noticed Holly when I came. Not that I would have done anything, but I might have been more prepared mentally.

"She's not married, did you know that?"

I nodded; not that he was paying attention. "Do you think it's wise to allow her to do that?" Snyder's words formed a question, but they came out of his mouth as an accusation. The room became deadly silent. Holly looked at us as though she'd just been shot. I think that's what did it for me.

There have been a number of unfortunate moments in my life when my mouth gets ahead of my brain. Even as I began to speak, I recognized this as one of those moments, but I couldn't seem to stop. "I have it on good authority that serving hot chocolate won't hurt the baby," I said.

Snyder shot to his feet, and his face lighted up so much I believe he would have triggered a Geiger counter. He looked around sharply and then leaned toward me, speaking in a confidential tone. "You'll be hearing more about this." Then, mercifully, he left.

I got up and walked toward the kitchen, where I could see Holly in the corner, leaning against a cupboard, her arms folded. Rose wore a grim expression. "I'm sorry," I said to both of them.

If Snyder's presence had subdued the atmosphere, his exit electrified it. Usually, each table at Grounds for Belief functions as its own little world, with little or no interchange between tables. But the evening's events had riveted everyone's attention. So, as I turned away from the counter, I saw every eye fixed on me.

"That's the kind of thing I come here to get away from," David said. An angry rumble through the room affirmed his sentiment.

"Me too," was all I could say. I started to see if anyone wanted to play Clue, but I detected a total lack of interest in games.

"OK," I said, "let's hear it. Everyone is upset, me included. Let's get it out in the open."

A few faces still looked at me, but most stared down at their tables.

"I'll say it," Lucas Enriquez spoke up. "What is this fixation so many religious people have with sex and sin? I think they use the word *sin* just as an excuse to look down on someone."

"That's what I think," said David. "*Sin* is just a word used to control other people." Others nodded or mumbled their agreement.

"Sin is passé?" I asked. "No longer relevant? Is that what you think?" David thrust his jaw forward, frowning—his "bulldog" look—and nodding vigorously.

"I don't know, I thought sin was *in*," I said.

"Huh?" a collective gasp rang through the room.

"The buzz on sin that I hear is strictly positive. You know: Treat yourself to something sinfully delicious! Tell a joke that's wickedly funny. Be a little naughty—have a little fun. Isn't that what you hear?" I asked.

David, slightly chagrined, said, "Well, if you put it *that* way."

"You've got to admit, sin gets great publicity." My approach clearly surprised them. "Let's be honest. Most of us find sin more interesting, more downright fun, than goodness. Isn't that true?" No one moved or spoke. "And the idea of righteousness—doesn't that sound, I don't know, not just stuffy but a little frightening too?"

"Now wait a minute," Lucas protested. "What are you saying?"

"Loosen up about this sin thing. You know, everyone needs to 'sow some wild oats, have a little fling, *live* a little.' Right?" I asked. Clearly, they were all stunned, so I dialed back a little bit. "Look, all I'm trying to say is that most of us secretly equate sin with fun and goodness with dullness. Am I wrong?

"Don't we actually celebrate little so-called sins like high-fat desserts," I continued, "fancy furniture, and expensive clothes? We like to flatter ourselves that we're beyond believing in that outdated concept called sin. After all, what is sin, anymore?"

Renee spoke up, "When I hear a politician who's preaching hate, that seems like sin to me."

"Or what about those corporate executives who looted their company, taking advantage of shareholders and employees? I think that's a sin." This from Mark MacKenzie, the accountant.

"So, you do think something like sin exists?" I asked, receiving a chorus of agreement in answer. "We just classify them differently, isn't that it?"

"How do you mean?" asked Lucas.

"Oh, for example, we prefer to identify sins as something others do, don't we?" A few "ooh's" told me to tread carefully. "We also rate our own transgressions by magnitude and by how common they are. So, Mark?" He looked up, surprised. "Suppose I cheat just a little on my expense account. Is that really a sin?" Mark's frown made it clear he classified that as a sin. But I went on. "After all, *everybody* does it—just chill, man. I mean, if it's a common occurrence, and the amounts are small, that's not really a sin, is it?"

David chimed in. "Come on, Mark, give a guy a break."

Renee said, "Well, I don't think loving someone is a sin. He should have left Holly alone."

"OK. Let's talk about that," I said. "So religious people classify every pleasure as sinful, especially when it comes to sex. Is that it?" I had found something they all agreed on.

· ☕ ·

Fornication, the old-fashioned word for casual sex, sounds fussy and silly and judgmental. *Don't get so excited,* we think, *it's just recreational sex.* Maybe. But if that's true, then why do two lovers who are actually in a relationship call "recreational sex" with someone else "cheating"? And when it happens to us, we know cheating is exactly what it is.

Whether we actually say the words or not, every sexual act implies a promise—a promise that the two in the relationship can trust each other in the deepest of ways, to be caring and respectful of each other's bodies and emotions. When one partner decides to have casual sex with someone else, that breaks the promise, and neither partner will be quite so open again, never again quite so trusting. Every future sexual act will be haunted by doubt, clouded by sorrow, inhibited by fear. So, "free love" inevitably leads to loving less freely.

No, loving someone isn't sin. Even the old pagan Plato understood that "pleasure is the bait of sin." Whatever pleasure-bait you think to gain, when you lie to me, steal my money or affections, wound me physically or kill my hopes, you betray my trust. Betraying a trust to get pleasure—now that's sin. Real sin, tear-your-heart-out, cry-your-eyes-out sin, always involves a betrayal of trust. Sin steals innocence and joy and wonder that cannot be replaced.

· ·

"No one here wants to condemn Holly or make her feel bad," I said. "We like her, and we don't like what Pastor Snyder did. That was wrong of him. But how do you feel about Holly's guy? It still takes two to make a baby. Some guy—we don't know who, and it's not really any of our business—got Holly pregnant, and he's leaving her all alone to deal with it. How do you feel about him?"

"I see what you mean," said David. "He did betray a trust. He hurt someone we all care for."

"To make matters worse, when we sin, we injure ourselves, as well," I said. "Elbert Hubbard said, 'Men are not punished *for* their sins, but *by* them.' "

"That's not so clear to me," David replied. "Looks like he got what he wanted, got off scott free. Granted, he acted like an idiot. But how did that hurt him?"

"For one thing, we all think he acted like an idiot, to use your words. His reputation suffered. But there's more to it than that . . ."

· ·

No one is more suspicious than a habitual cheater. Because they know their own cheating ways, they expect everyone else to cheat them too. So the liar expects to be lied to; the confidence artist expects to be scammed; the thief fears his possessions will be stolen. The adulterer fears his spouse will be unfaithful. Each violation of trust eats away at our own humanity, erodes our hope and optimism, and cripples our ability to enjoy life.

And it makes it more likely we will hurt others. Nothing is more dangerous than a wounded animal. The most ghastly serial killers almost always come from horrific abusive backgrounds themselves. None of us is beyond lashing out in pain and hurting even those closest to us.

When you get down to it, sin always has consequences—real grief, real pain, disease, even death. Do you doubt it? Talk to the child of an alcoholic, still bearing the emotional scars of abuse into adulthood. Go to a third-world slum and look into the dead eyes of a child prostitute, eyes bereft of all joy and light and innocence. Look in the mirror and remember when someone abused your trust, repaid your kindness with cruelty, exploited your openness.

· ☕ ·

I faced a pretty solemn group now. "John Donne got it right. No human being is an island, isolated from others, able to act with impunity, without consequences for anyone else. Even if we could do that, sin would still be deadly."

"What do you mean?" asked Renee.

"Have you ever heard the story of *The Picture of Dorian Gray?*" I asked.

"Tell us," said Lucas.

· ☕ ·

In the story, the handsome young title character, Dorian Gray, commissions a portrait of himself. Taken by his own comeliness in the portrait, Dorian makes a deal with the devil: Every sin he commits will be recorded on the portrait, while his real face remains young and handsome.

Believing himself immune from the consequences of his actions, Dorian Gray descends into evil: betraying the trust of a sweet young woman; committing a murder; driving a friend to suicide. To others, Dorian appears as youthful and handsome as when the portrait was painted. He's the only one who can see the progressive ugliness of his soul, as reflected by the tell-tale portrait hidden in a private place.

Eventually he can no longer abide the frightful accusation the portrait represents. Believing the painting to be the source of his unhappiness, Dorian decides to destroy it. Locking himself inside the room, he makes to slash the canvas with a knife. His servants hear a scream from the room. Eventually they break in, to find a most curious situation. "When they entered, they found hanging upon the wall a splendid portrait of their master as they had last seen him, in all the wonder of his exquisite youth and beauty. Lying on the floor was a dead man, in evening dress, with a knife in his heart. He was withered, wrinkled, and loathsome of visage. It was not till they had examined the rings that they recognized who it was."

· ☕ ·

"Wow," said David.

"That's creepy," Renee added.

"You see, even if our sins affected no one else," I said, "each of us has our Dorian Gray portrait." I paused, and wide eyes returned my gaze from every table. "You know what I mean. When we wake in the quiet hours before dawn, that portrait looms before us in the darkness. Etched on it we see the record of every mean, cruel, and despicable act. Every twisted motive haunts our memories. Though carefully concealed from others, we cannot escape it."

All around me I saw ashen faces. Renee wiped away a tear. Holly and Rose hadn't left the kitchen, but no sounds came from behind me either.

"No. Sin isn't chic," I said. "Cruelty and pain never come into fashion. No matter how jaded, how sophisticated, how blasé we may wish to think ourselves, we still know evil exists. We feel it in our bones and see its deadly effects in our own lives. Whatever we may say, we know that we live as broken people, in a broken world, and sense deep within that it ought not to be this way.

"What Pastor Snyder did was wrong—it was a betrayal of trust. That's what sin is and what sin does. We all know it, because we all have done it and have had it done to us."

"That's depressing," said Mark MacKenzie. "So OK, so we agree sin is real. Now what? What can we do about it?"

I looked at the clock and saw we still had time before closing. "There are several answers," I said. "As bad as sin is, there's a way to keep it from weighing us down."

"There is?" said David. "I'd like to hear that."

"Well, it starts like this. . . ."

Detour From the Guilt Trip

. . . . .

"Did you ever say something and almost immediately feel like a fool?" I asked.

"You mean what you said to Pastor Snyder?" asked Lucas, with a touch of suspicion.

"No. No, no, no. That may have been a mistake, but it was not either needlessly cruel or painful," I said. "No, I mean just inexcusable. Something like I did to my wife the other day . . ."

. ☕ .

I don't remember the exact words. I do remember feeling wronged and therefore quite justified as I said them. Then, as the seconds passed in silence, the words echoed and re-echoed in my mind. An aching emptiness struck my heart as I recognized the cruelty I had committed against my wife, Mavis, who deserved only kindness from me.

In an attempt at defense, I could protest that "I did not mean to," but it would be only half true. Sometimes, in moments of pain, hurt, or anger, I lash out, wanting someone else to hurt too; wanting someone to suffer instead of me; wanting to exact revenge on a cruel world. I rarely intend to hurt my spouse, my child, my friend, or some random stranger in the process. I just want someone to pay, and whoever gets in the way of my anger does pay. This time, my wife paid. I regretted my anger, and the cruel words, but nothing could call them back. Probably you know that sense of despair at what you've done. Perhaps you, too, have wondered where to find hope when we do wrong.

· ☕ ·

"Everybody makes mistakes," said Lucas. "Don't be too tough on yourself."

"Oh, I'm not," I said. "Let's be clear: I'm not talking about mistakes, about unintended bumps and bruises. Sure, in this broken world we live in, things go wrong in spite of our best efforts. No matter how painful the consequences, these mistakes and accidents must be excused."

"Wait a minute," said David. "You're saying that if someone accidentally destroys my new car—?"

"If it's an accident, it's an accident," I said. "How can you hold it against him?"

"If he got drunk and wrecked it?"

"Now, getting drunk isn't accidental," I said. "That's a different matter."

"OK, OK. I got you." David seemed satisfied.

"We only injure ourselves further by harboring bitterness about things beyond anyone's control," I said, holding out my hands, palm up. "No, I'm talking about deliberate, intentional cruelty. True wrongs, inexcusable offenses. We've all done those wrongs, those cruel, unpardonable deeds."

"Well, I mean, it's not like you actually killed someone." This from Lucas.

"No, I've never killed anyone, and neither have you. We've never stood guard at a concentration camp, we've never stolen someone's life savings, never driven anyone to suicide. Still, in a sudden burst of anger, or cold-blooded spite, I have killed someone's hope, made a child feel worthless, or repaid a friend's kindness with cruelty, just as I did with my wife.

"Where do we go? Where do you and I, the guard from Auschwitz, the brutal killers of Kosovo, and all the other guilty people, go to find peace? Where can we find hope when our actions cannot be justified?"

"So tell us," said David.

"Well, I cannot find peace and hope for you, but I can share my journey of discovery."

• ☕ •

My journey started with science. I hoped that science and logic could offer some relief. But, to my dismay, science only compounded my problem. For science warns me that I cannot bring the dead back to life, cannot turn back the clock and relive the crucial moments. The natural world acts by the inexorable law of cause and effect: Every action provokes an equal and opposite reaction. The ripples from every cruel deed surge outward in ever larger circles through our lives. The angry bell can't be unrung.

Even worse, nature doesn't care. As scientist Richard Dawkins says, "Nature is not cruel, only pitilessly indifferent." Nature ignores my guilt, offers no relief for my anguish.

• ☕ •

"Well, I wouldn't look to science, anyway," said David.

"Where should I look then?" I asked.

Mark MacKenzie spoke up. "What about Buddhism? I've heard they're pretty peaceful."

"Sounds promising," I said. "The calm of meditation attracts me, and I've always wondered if maybe the smile of the Buddha hints at some hidden source of serenity.

"It looks good on the surface," I said. "But lurking beneath that calm you'll find the belief in samsara—the wheel of life and endless rebirth."

"Yeah, one of my classmates was talking about that," Renee said. "Isn't that reincarnation?"

"Yes," I said. "And according to samsara, we're reborn to pay for the sins of the previous life. Every action in this life becomes part of your karma in the next. This guarantees that every evil, thoughtless, harmful deed done in this life must be paid for in the next life—and the next, and the next—retribution without end. Wrongdoing cannot be escaped or mitigated, only paid for."

Renee made a face. "Eewww! That's really mean."

"It's not by accident that from Buddhism comes the proverb, 'The wheel of justice grinds slow, but it grinds exceeding fine.'"

"But they seem so peaceful when they meditate," Renee said.

"In their meditation, Buddhists seek to become 'one with nature,' " I said.

"But you just said that nature doesn't care about suffering," Mark reminded us. "So to become 'one with nature' means we won't care either."

"Exactly," I said. "The peace you discern is the peace of indifference. I don't know about you, but I need something more than indifference when I do wrong. Or do we just drift further and further apart?"

"That can't be right," Mark said.

"So, what does that leave us with?" asked David.

"Religion," said Lucas. "Religion is all that's left."

"Yes, but which one?" said David. "After all, most wars have been fought in the name of religion."

"Maybe we'll talk about that some other night," I said. "For now, I'm still looking for relief when I do wrong. And yes, Lucas, only religion remains. But which religion?"

· ☕ ·

"There is one God, and Mohammad is his prophet." That statement stands at the center of Islam. Mohammad the prophet dealt severely with guilt: He waged war, took captives and made them slaves, and executed enemies. And Muslim poet Omar Khayyam warned,

The Moving Finger writes; and, having writ,
Moves on: nor all your Piety nor Wit
Shall lure it back to cancel half a Line,
Nor all your Tears wash out a Word of it.

That means the record of wrongdoing cannot be expunged.

And Muslim Sharia law deals sternly with infractions. A thief may have his hand amputated; adultery calls for stoning to death. Allah may be merciful, and many Muslims may be kind neighbors, but I find nothing in Islam that gives hope for the truly guilty. Can there be no hope for reconciliation, once I do wrong?

Finding no hope in Islam, I moved on to Judaism. The Law, whether the Ten Commandments or the 613 *mitzvot*, the *gezeirah*, the *takkanah*, a *minhag*—rings within rings of law stand at the center of Judaism. Absolute, fixed, and permanent, the Law identifies violators and prescribes punishment. It protects us from predators and maintains civil society. But the Law offers no hope for lawbreakers, for those who, in Bart Simpson's phrase, "What thou shalt not, I shalt did." The Law punishes lawbreakers and offers no mercy, no hope to those without excuse. Yet, it's especially when there's no excuse for my misdeeds that I need hope. My search continued.

. ☕ .

"Wait a minute," said David. "You're not going to tell me that Christianity holds some hope for wrongdoers, are you?"

"What's at the center of Christianity?" I asked.

"I don't know, the Sermon on the Mount?" David replied.

"That's a great idea, but not the very center. What's the one thing in Christianity that, if you eliminated it, the religion would cease to exist?"

"That would have to be Jesus," Lucas said.

"Exactly. The 'Christ' in Christianity," I agreed. "And what is central even in the life of Christ?"

"You mean the Crucifixion, don't you?" asked Renee.

"Yes, and if you've seen even a trailer for Mel Gibson's film, *The Passion,* you know that Jesus, an innocent man, was condemned to a grisly, bloody, painful death. Yet, even after Roman soldiers had hammered nails through His hands and hoisted the cross upright, He cried out to God, 'Father, forgive them for they do not know what they are doing.' "

"And that's the remedy for sin, for doing wrong," Mark said in a low voice. "Forgiveness."

"When you see it, you realize that's what you're looking for. A dying man who can forgive his torturers can be counted on to forgive anyone, surely," I said. "That's the kind of forgiveness I need, the kind that comes when I cannot repay an infinite debt, cannot unsay the cruel words, cannot undo the undoable. It's the kind of forgiveness that only comes into play when all excuses have been exhausted, when only our acknowledgment of wrongdoing and the guilty feeling in our gut remain."

"That's it?" said David, obviously alarmed. "Someone hurts you and you just forgive them?"

"Well, when you hurt someone, do you want forgiveness?" I asked.

David didn't answer, just sat, frowning, and chewing on his lip. Finally he spoke. "Forgiveness, no conditions?"

"The only condition is that we open ourselves fully to forgiveness, both to receive and to give. For we receive forgiveness only as we extend it to others. 'Forgive us for doing wrong, as we forgive others' [Matthew 6:12, CEV]. In our cold, unforgiving world, when we let forgiveness flow out to others, the healing stream purges us of our own torment. But if we hoard it, trap it in a cold heart, it freezes solid as stone."

"I don't know if I can do that," David said.

"None of us can," I said, "not easily, and not without help. Forgiveness does not come naturally. When at fault, we don't like to humble ourselves and ask for it, and when wronged, we don't want to give it. Since it does not come naturally, we must experience forgiveness before we can offer it to others."

"So, what does all this have to do with the Crucifixion? If sin can be forgiven, why did Jesus die for it?" David asked.

"Good questions," I said, "but we're running late, and Rose needs to close up. But the short answer about the Cross and forgiveness is that it has to start somewhere. We needed Someone to come and show us how. Jesus did that on the cross."

"Why don't we hear more about forgiveness from people like Pastor Snyder?" Lucas asked.

"Another good question, but it's time to leave. Just remember this: Forgiveness is the only remedy for those of us who do wrong, and there's only one place to find it. Of all the world's religions and philosophies, only Christianity places the need for forgiveness—and the remedy—at its very center."

Enterprise, I Have a Problem!

• • • • •

I try to avoid arguments about religion," I said.

"Very funny," said David, "but it's your turn. Everyone else has shared. *Star Trek* or *Star Wars*?"

It looked to be true. Even the usually imperturbable Scrabble game in the corner had stopped, all the players now looking at me. "Everyone has shared?" I said, looking desperately for a way out. Then I spotted Caroline, who came seldom and almost never spoke in the group. "What about Caroline?" Quiet when not singing, I felt certain she hadn't joined in.

"I said Skywalker and Vader—*Star Wars*," Caroline volunteered. "In fact, I started the debate," she said, giving a short, sharp nod that said, "So there." Caroline had started the debate? What a shock. I knew about her interest in music, yes. But science fiction? I mean, who knew?

So, in my best Patrick Stewart imitation—I can't do Shatner for anything—I intoned, "These are the voyages of the starship . . ."

"Aha!" Mark MacKenzie exclaimed. "I knew it! He's been a Trekkie all along!"

Rose had leaned in from the kitchen, and, wiping her hands on her apron, she asked, "What's a Trekkie? And do I need to call the exterminator?"

Again, Caroline surprised me by speaking up. "You know, a fan of the *Star Trek* TV series and movies?"

Rose paused for a moment, even her hands still for once. She turned her gaze to me and opened her mouth as if to speak, but then appeared

54

to think better of it. She shook her head slightly and, with a dismissive wave of her hand, walked back into the kitchen.

"OK, you found me out. I'm a closet Trekkie."

"And at your age," Mark said in mock disapproval.

"All right, yes, even in my advancing years, I like to imagine myself as the captain (what else?) of the *Enterprise*." Again I switched to my Patrick Stewart voice. "Boldly going where no one has gone before, seeking new life forms . . ." I stopped there, because this admission seemed to have struck everyone as unspeakably funny. I came to this conclusion not because of the volume of the laughter, though Caroline giggled and Lucas gave out a belly laugh. No, it had more to do with David's sly smile and Mark—and the rest—shaking, red-faced and silent.

When she could breathe again, Erica said, "That's the worst Shatner imitation I've ever heard."

Even as I spoke, I realized my mistake, but the words came out anyway. "But I was doing Patrick Stewart," I said. The resulting explosion of laughter bruised my already wounded pride further. Rose returned to assess the damage, but when she saw everyone laughing uncontrollably except me, she put her hands on her hips, pursed her lips, and with a quick look at me, gave a short, despairing shake of her head and marched back into the kitchen.

Eventually, the atmosphere stabilized. Risking further derision, I said, "I did have one big problem with it though. I mean, maybe I'm the only one, but I always wondered, how would you know a new life form when you encountered it?"

"But they did it nearly every episode," Erica said, laughing again.

"No. No. He's right," Mark said, sobering slightly. "Because the life forms they found were so different, like . . . the crystal entity."

"Or there was that space-traversing manta-ray-type thing that nursed on the ship's energy . . . what? Doesn't anyone remember that episode?" David asked, looking around sharply. Apparently no one did. "That was so cool."

"Anyway, they encountered intelligent life in many forms—" I began.

"—and always identified them within the allotted fifty-two minutes of broadcast time," said Mark, ever the accountant.

"Why did they want to find new life forms, anyway?" Lucas Enriquez asked. "Seems like they always ran into trouble."

"I think the theory was that they sought out new life forms at least partially because they wanted superior technology," Mark explained. "The trouble with that is that advanced technology requires advanced intelligence. And both superior technology and superior intelligence can be dangerous to those less advanced."

"But that's exactly where they lost me," I said. "I mean, it seems pretty logical, doesn't it? It takes advanced intelligence to design and manufacture advanced technology. So, what was the most advanced device on *Star Trek*?"

"I always wanted the transporter myself," said Mark.

"I'd like to get my hands on a phaser, maybe a photon torpedo," added David.

"It's Data, isn't it?" Erica asked, looking surprised at her own discovery. "Data, the android. He's the most advanced technology they had."

"And it took a genius to design and build him," Mark said, "Dr. Noonian Sung." He thought for a second. "Yeah, it has to be Data. I loved it when he played Sherlock Holmes on the holodeck."

"He played the violin!" said Erica, who had been known to pick up a violin herself.

"He even wrote a poem to his cat, Spot." This from Renee.

"But Data makes the problem worse," I said.

"How's that?" asked Mark.

"Who was more advanced, Data or Captain Picard? Or, come to think about it, was Data more or less advanced than his cat, Spot? Be careful. Remember, Spot could feel, taste—even reproduce. Data couldn't do any of those simple things."

· ☕ ·

Although Data enjoyed specific advantages over his human shipmates, he—and they—recognized that human beings exhibit far more complexity than androids. So Data, despite all of his marvelous capabilities, aspired to be human, because to be human is superior to being an android. At the very same time, the Trek world leaves no doubt that, although Data resulted from a process of meticulous design and purposeful manufacture, human beings resulted from a very long series of improbable accidents.

Yes, they use the word *evolution,* and they believe there are "forces" at work—adaptation and natural selection—but they all depend upon mutations, and a mutation is an accident. More specifically, when the DNA in a cell replicates or makes a copy of itself, sometimes mistakes are made—random mistakes, that is important—and the copy differs from the original. Most of these mistakes are detrimental, even lethal, but a very few actually make things a little better. In any event, every mutation, good and bad, results from a random accident.

· ☕ ·

"So, we're asked to believe Data needs a genius designer, but the lovely Deanna Troi resulted from an almost infinite chain of fortunate accidents," Mark said, pensively.

"Whatever happened to 'advanced technologies come from advanced intelligence'?" I asked. "And the further you go, the worse it gets. Come with me, in my imagination, as members of the 'away team.' "

"Away team? Are we going somewhere?" Rose, who had been listening from behind the counter, asked.

"That's what they called a special group of crew members chosen to explore new planets. They went away from the ship, so they were the 'away team,' " Mark explained. "So, tell us more . . ."

· ☕ ·

On a desert planet, we encounter a large complex of buildings, inhabited only by lizards. Inside this building, elaborate holograms recount the planet's history. But here comes my problem again.

On the one hand, we believe the buildings, the technology, and the holograms testify of the intelligence of the planet's former inhabitants. But in the world of *Star Trek,* we're supposed to believe that the lizards, every cell of which exhibits more complexity than all the technological relics we have found, "just happened."

Maybe it's a failure of imagination. I can imagine human beings making a starship like the *Enterprise,* but I just can't look at shingled scales on a butterfly's wing and say, "This is the product of chance." How does it make sense that while my car took months to design and build, my body and the trees outside and migrating birds and the dancing honeybees and great whales in the sea and Bengal tigers and kangaroos and even little finches—just happened?

·☕·

"Sure, but if you talk like this, especially in my school—" Renee was in her senior year at an elite small college "—you can expect to be ridiculed. Most teachers, scientists, and philosophers, even some clergy, will call you foolish, superstitious, stupid, or worse. Not to mention your classmates."

"That's why I took notice a couple of years ago when British philosopher Antony Flew, who for more than fifty years had been a champion of atheism, announced that he had come to believe in intelligent design," I said.

"I'm not familiar with the name," Mark said.

·☕·

It's been an interesting journey for Antony Flew. The son of a Methodist minister, he became an atheist as a teenager. As a young adult, he became involved in a weekly religious forum at Oxford called the Socratic Club, led by C. S. Lewis. Like Flew, Lewis embraced atheism in his youth but had become a leading Christian thinker and writer by the time the two met. That encounter led, not to Flew's conversion but to his writing the paper that would become "Falsification and Theology." That publication heralded Flew's arrival as a leading promoter of atheism. In 1984, Flew published "The Presumption of Atheism." There he argued that, rather than atheists disproving the existence of God, the burden of proof should be on those who argue that God exists.

But Flew now believes science has met that burden of proof. In a new video titled *Has Science Discovered God?* he declares that biological studies of DNA have "shown, by the almost unbelievable complexity of the arrangements which are needed to produce [life], that intelligence must have been involved." Has the minister's son come full circle? Not quite.

"I'm thinking of a God very different from the God of the Christian and far and away from the God of Islam, because both are depicted as omnipotent Oriental despots, cosmic Saddam Husseins," he said. At the same time, he admitted, "It could be a person in the sense of a being that has intelligence and a purpose, I suppose."

"So, he believes in Creation but not God?" David asked.

"More like he believes in intelligent design, and some sort of designer, sounds like to me," said Mark.

"I think Mark has it about right. Flew now believes he was wrong all those years in supposing God did not exist. He now believes that the complexity of some of the fundamental structures of life demands intelligent design."

"Well, maybe he's wrong about the Bible's depiction of God as an 'Oriental despot,' too," said Lucas.

"Maybe," I agreed. "But that's a step each individual has to think about for themselves. For me, it seems that the infinite intelligence required to design the intricacies of DNA, and to originate the complex sequences of the human genome, must also be the lover of beauty that painted the scales on the butterfly's wing and made Deanna Troi not just intelligent but winsome."

"Just try selling that on campus," said Renee. "My teachers claim that they believe in science, whereas intelligent design is a belief in magic."

"I'm sure they do. But it was evolutionist and science fiction writer Arthur C. Clarke who said, 'Any sufficiently advanced technology is indistinguishable from magic.' It seems to me that any being intelligent enough to invent the human genome might just be capable of feats 'indistinguishable from magic.' "

"You're saying the Intelligent Designer is so advanced, and that's why scientists see it as 'magic'?" asked Mark.

"I'm saying it's worth thinking about. I'm saying that maybe that old story is right when it says that we humans were made in the likeness of God. And it's that 'likeness' that makes us want to 'boldly go where no one has gone before,' " I said. "Whether we're following that quest into the remote corners of the galaxy in our imagination or seeking to decode the mysteries in our DNA."

"Maybe that's the secret behind tales like *Star Trek*. Because we seek not just new technology but also to know and understand the intelligent beings that made the technology. And we seek not just new *life forms* but also to know and understand the Designer of life."

Goldilocks and God

* * * *

Mark MacKenzie brought The Settlers of Catan the next week. I enjoy the game, even though he regularly humbles me. On this night, it looked as though I might actually build the longest road and earn the two points for that accomplishment. Mark ended up with the largest army and won anyway. David had pulled up his chair to watch the carnage, and the expression on his face told me he wanted something.

As soon as our game finished, David said, "Been thinking."

"Sometimes it can't be avoided," I said, smiling.

" 'Bout last week. What you said. Intelligent design and all."

"And—"

"And, well, I agree about intelligent design—I mean, life's too complex just to be an accident."

I knew something wasn't sitting right with him, and I said so.

"Exactly," David said.

I felt impatient, but I knew he'd come to it eventually.

"Well, I know this might be considered terrible, but I've gotta ask," David said. By now, everyone was leaning forward. "Why one?"

"I'm sorry. I don't understand the question," I said.

"Why just one designer?" David said.

"I get it, I think," Mark volunteered. "Large engineering projects—oh, the Sears Tower, for example—employ a team of designers. David's asking, 'Does the theory of intelligent design require a single designer?' Is that right?"

"Pretty much," David said. "Let's face it, if there's one Designer, that pretty much makes Him God. Why can't there be lots of designers instead of just one?"

"But that would mean lots of gods," Renee said, clearly troubled.

"Goldilocks," I said.

"Huh?" came the collective reply.

"It's the Goldilocks question, only applied to God," I said. Still not seeing any indication of understanding, I went on. "Goldilocks kept looking for whatever was 'just right.' So, when it comes to the question of gods, how many are 'just right'?"

"Well, it could be any number, couldn't it?" Renee said.

"Many different numbers have been suggested," I said.

"Well, there's got to be a practical limit," said Mark, who did, after all, crunch numbers as easily as the rest of us swatted flies.

"What's the highest number of gods you've heard about?" asked Lucas.

"Three-hundred and thirty million," I said.

"Wait a minute. Did you say thirty-three followed by *seven zeroes?*" Mark apparently found it hard to fathom.

"That's the highest number I've heard," I said, "but some people believe in even more."

"How is that possible?" asked David, "and who are the people who believe in so many?"

. ☕ .

It's called pantheism, and although it dates back to ancient times, it has become more popular lately. In ancient times, people saw mountains and rivers and plants and animals and decided that these things had "made themselves." Pantheism, which literally means "God is everything," believes just that: God is everywhere, in everything, is everything. God is in every blade of grass. God is in flowers and trees and worms and fish and birds and—you get the idea. The god in the flower designs and animates the flower; the god in the river designs and moves the river, and so on.

"But wait a minute," Mark said. "If god is in fact in everything, and if everything is god, then there is no god. The god in the dandelion and the god in the bluegrass are at constant war with one another."

"Uh huh. It's like the old story of a man inspecting a beautiful estate," I said. "As he viewed the dignified house, beautiful gardens, and lovely stream, he said, 'This is truly God's country.' To which the estate owner, painfully aware of the labor and expense that had gone into it, replied, 'Yes, well, you should have seen it when God had it to Himself.'

"That's the god of pantheism he was referring to. Leave the universe to the god of pantheism, and you get 'nature, red in tooth and claw,' but no God you can talk to."

"So, even if this pantheism is true, it's essentially worthless," David said. "What other choices do we have?"

After pantheism—God in everything—comes the idea of many gods. Hinduism is reputed to have as many as 330,000,000 gods. Egyptians, Greeks, Romans, Mayas, Vikings, Druids—most ancient cultures had many gods, one for every situation. However, when you have many gods, they fight one another. For every wise Odin, who orders the universe, there is a mischievous Loki just looking to mess things up.

"In that case, many gods are worse than no god at all," said Mark.

"Because they're always fighting one another. I see that," said Lucas.

"Yes. If there are many gods in conflict with one another, we're better off if we can escape their notice," I said. "Because whichever one we choose to ally ourselves with, to worship and seek help from, there will be another god—and sometimes many gods—opposed to us."

"On the battlefield, the more parties involved, the greater the chance for collateral damage," said David, our former marine.

"And that's what happened in all the ancient stories of multiple gods, wherever they were. Human beings became the collateral damage when gods came into conflict," I said.

"Your Goldilocks would be out of luck," Mark pointed out, "because no single god would ever meet all her needs. None would be 'just right.' Many gods turns out to be no god at all."

"OK," said Renee, "what does that leave us with?"

· ☕ ·

Because the world contains both good and evil, light and dark, yin and yang, some religions—some forms of Zoroastrianism and early Taoism are two examples—believe there must be *two* gods. We call this sort of belief "dualism." And it has a lot of appeal. For example, it removes the need to wrestle with the question: "If God is good, why is there so much evil and suffering?" Dualism takes care of that by believing in a god of evil, for want of a better term. The two gods of dualism are locked in an eternal struggle, and neither has the power to win. But dualism's strength is also its greatest flaw.

To believe in dualism, Goldilocks has to believe that evil and good possess equal strength, equal appeal, and equal validity. Trouble is, they just don't. Light a match on a dark night, and it can be visible for miles. A light bulb can brighten a dark room. But you can't find a "dark bulb" to darken a bright one. Evil, cold, darkness—none of these exists on its own. Each exists only as a negation or absence of its opposite. And that's the problem of dualism. The evil god can't make it on his own. He needs the good god to oppose. He also needs the good qualities to motivate his followers.

· ☕ ·

"Wait a minute," David said. "I'm beginning to like this dualism idea. Why can't there be a 'dark force'?"

"Yes, tell us, Obi Wan, tell us of the dark side," Lucas intoned. I raised an eyebrow and nodded at him once.

"The problem is that no one does evil for its own sake," I said. "We only do bad things to get good things. People steal money so they can enjoy the goods that money can buy. Pleasure itself is good. It's *how* we get it that can be evil."

"I see it," said Mark. "If the 'evil god' can only motivate his followers with what the 'good god' provides, then he, the 'evil god,' is dependent upon the 'good god.' And if dependent, then not as powerful."

"That's where the whole thing breaks down," I said, "because if the good force is inherently stronger than the bad one, then the battle will not go on forever. Goldilocks discovers that two gods offers no real choice, since eventually the stronger, better force will win out, and there will be only one."

"Then that has to be the answer," said Renee. "In the end, only one God will satisfy our spiritual Goldilocks. Only one God will be 'just right.' "

"And that's why," Lucas chimed in, "the three largest religions are 'monotheistic,' believing in one God."

"Jews, Muslims, and Christians don't agree on much, but they all agree on this idea of one God. If there is a God, then He must be One," I said. "Not two, not many. And while His power may be seen in every living thing, they are not Him, and He is not them, for He must be One.

"That is," I added, "if there is a God."

"Well, OK, I can see that," said David. "But if there is only one good God, then what about evil? If there is no evil 'god,' then is evil a force?"

Rose had come out and busied herself clearing the tables. Mark had long since put away The Settlers of Catan.

"You're asking if such a thing as a devil exists, then, aren't you?" I answered.

"I guess I am," said David. "How about it?"

Rose looked up and said, in no uncertain tones, "I need to close up because I need to get home on time tonight. So, that discussion, whatever it is, will have to wait."

The Devil, You Say

* * * * *

You said you were a Trekkie," David protested.

Grounds for Belief had barely gotten under way the next week when David accosted me with his question about the devil. I said something about Darth Vader, which elicited his protest.

"Yes, I prefer *Star Trek*, but you asked me about the devil. Can you think of a more devilish character than Darth Vader?" I asked.

"I see your point."

"I mean, from the moment Darth Vader, dressed in glossy black, bursts onto a screen full of white-clad star troopers, you have no doubts this is one bad guy," I said. "Even when we don't actually see him . . ."

"We hear that mechanical breathing sound—that's so cool," David said.

"And so scary." This from Caroline, who had slipped in unnoticed.

"That's what makes it cool," David replied.

"And there's that mask he wears; it creeps me out just to look at him," said Renee. "It's still scary, more than thirty years later, because the director, George Lucas, gave Vader that mask. So, when we look at Vader, instead of a face, we see what resembles a black robotlike death's head fused to an oversize Nazi coal-scuttle helmet," I explained. "So he's using symbols that frighten us—the machinelike robot, the color black, the death's head, and Nazis, all rolled into one."

"And he no sooner strides onto the scene than he crushes that guy with his bare hands. He's one evil dude," said David.

"And so when Obi-Wan Kenobi describes Vader to the young Luke Skywalker, saying 'He's more machine now than man; twisted and evil,' we feel it's the truth," I said. "His name, his voice, his appearance, his actions—everything about Darth Vader marks him as the personification of evil. Would you call him 'the devil of *Star Wars*'?"

"I would," Caroline said, nodding thoughtfully, her clasped hands in her lap.

"I suppose, but—" said David.

"But he repents in the end," said Renee.

"Actually, *Star Wars* doesn't accept the idea of a being called the devil," I said. "And most people agree. Public surveys continually reveal that fewer and fewer people believe in a being called the devil. Oh, most of us agree that evil surely exists, but a real *being,* who's plotting, scheming, tempting, seducing? A person seeking our destruction? *Nah. "*

"Well, does there have to be a devil?" David asked.

"Maybe not, but for someone very few believe in, the devil sure pops up a lot in conversation," I said.

"What do you mean? I don't talk about him," said Caroline.

"Really? Every culture has a name for him. A little strange for a non-existent person, don't you think? And then, proverbs and figures of speech about the devil abound. You know, 'You've got to give the devil his due.' 'Speak of the devil, and he appears.'

"No matter how much we wish him to disappear, Old Nick just won't seem to go away," I continued. "Even *Star Wars* personified evil in Darth Vader. It's as though it's not enough to recognize the dark side of the Force—we have to make it *personal.*"

"I remember Obi-Wan Kenobi telling Luke, 'Vader was seduced by the dark side of the Force,' " said Mark. "But a force doesn't seduce. That takes a person."

"But why just the dark side?" asked David.

"I never thought of that," said Lucas. "We don't even have a name for 'the bright side' of the Force. Yoda and Obi-Wan Kenobi are both Jedi masters, but we don't think of them as personifying goodness. Yet we immediately feel that Darth Vader personifies evil. Can you explain that?"

"I don't know," I said. "That's a pretty tall order. I have some ideas I could share." I looked at their faces. No one objected, so I started in.

· ☕ ·

We're all afraid of the dark. We learn to cope with it as we grow up, but fear of the dark is just another word for fear of the unknown. At the edge of illumination, where sight dims and shadow begins, we enter the dark unknown, and if we are honest, we feel a thrill of fright. Seeking what cannot be seen, we peer into the emptiness, wondering what awaits us. Does a malevolent entity inhabit the deepest shadows, ready to spring if we stray too far? Or is it a realm of yawning emptiness, of profound nothingness—what some call "the abyss"?

Friedrich Nietzsche said, "When you look into the abyss, the abyss also looks into you." I think we sense the abyss looking into us. It draws and repels us at the same time. We fear the dark, the emptiness, not knowing whether something, someone, lurks there, yet it fascinates us. On the verge, we hear the seductive call, "Give yourself to the dark side."

· ☕ ·

"That part of the movie always gives me the chills," Caroline said.

"Yet you enjoy it, don't you?" I asked.

"Well—kind of—I guess," she said, cringing a little as she said it.

"Then you recognize the appeal of that 'something' in the dark, don't you?"

She didn't say a word, just shivered a little.

"That's the danger. In real life, some yield to that seductive voice, getting involved with satanism and the occult." I looked at a group of pretty sober faces. "I think most of us fear that sort of entanglement, and rather than fall victim to it ourselves—afraid to look into the abyss and perhaps sensing someone within the abyss looking back into us—we just deny the devil's existence."

"Sounds good to me," said Renee.

"If the devil does exist, that's just what he'd want us to do," I said.

"Wait a minute! How can that be true?" David wasn't buying.

"For the sake of discussion, suppose the devil exists," I said. "A being devoted to your destruction, he's your worst enemy, and he will attack you. What would he want to do first? You're a marine, David, what's the most important edge in battle?"

"Firepower."

"Even more important than that? What if you don't get to use your firepower?"

"Gotcha! *Surprise!*"

"And the greatest surprise is not even knowing your enemy exists!" said Mark. "Like any clever adversary, he'd want to keep his plans and purposes secret. The less you know about how he plans to harm you, the more likely his plans will succeed."

"So, from the devil's point of view," here Lucas took up the thought, "the best option would be for you *not* to believe he existed. After all, why bother with someone who doesn't exist?"

"If the devil exists, he's pleased about how few people worry about him," I said.

"But what if he couldn't convince you he doesn't exist?" Lucas asked.

"Oh, that's easy," said David. "If you can convince your enemy that he has no chance, if you're overwhelmingly powerful, he won't fight."

"Resistance is futile," Mark intoned.

"Right. That's 'the Borg,' from *Star Trek*," Caroline said.

"The idea is to remove your hope so that you'll go quietly, without a struggle," Mark said.

"There's one more alternative," I said. "What if he can't get you to think of him as either all-powerful or nonexistent? What would the next best alternative be?"

"Harmless," said David, "so you wouldn't expect an attack. Just another way of being surprised."

"Even better than harmless is comical," I said.

"You mean the guy with the goatee and horns dressed in red tights?" asked Mark.

I nodded. "Sure—a buffoon, a bumbler, harmless—that image would do nicely. The last thing he'd want you to think is that he's clever, cunning, and subtle. For example, there's nothing subtle about Darth Vader, but an old story describes the devil just that way, as very, very subtle. And think about it. Of course it could be coincidence, but popular perceptions of the devil—nonexistent, overwhelmingly powerful, comical, and harmless—all of those images would suit a clever, subtle being just fine." I could see everyone thinking seriously about what I'd just said, so I waited a moment before I added, "If he exists."

"But that's where we started," said David, sounding a little frustrated. "Does he exist?"

"My opinion? I can't prove the devil exists," I said, "but the fact that human beings insist on making evil personal leads me to believe it's likely that he does. On a general, abstract level, it's easy for us to deny his existence. But when we get down to specifics, it's more difficult. The devil, it seems, is always in the details. Every culture has a name for the devil, and I think that when we gaze into the abyss, most of us sense *someone* gazing back."

"I don't like that at all," said Caroline.

"Me either," I said. "I'd like to think no evil being, no cunning adversary, no personal devil actually exists. It would be comforting. But then I remember what Darth Vader said to Luke Skywalker."

"I know this," Lucas spoke up. "He said 'You don't know the power of the dark side. I must obey my master.' "

Why Would God Create a Devil?

• • • • •

But if there is a God who is good and a devil, how did this happen?" David looked puzzled. "I mean, why would a good God create a devil?"

I hadn't expected much of a crowd at Grounds for Belief that night. It was one of those long summer evenings where delicious aromas fill the air from distant charcoal grills and people of all ages like to get in another round of miniature golf, one more hour at the swimming pool, or just walk along grassy trails. Even the sun seems to linger in the sky, reluctant to bid farewell to the day's attractions.

"And if God didn't create the devil, then where'd Old Nick come from?" added Lucas.

"And why didn't God just kill the devil and avoid all this suffering?" This from Caroline.

"Why not just make it impossible for the devil to do wrong?" asked Renee.

"While He was at it, why didn't God make it impossible for *us* to do wrong?" said Mark. "Save everyone a lot of trouble."

"Wow, that's a lot of questions. I may actually have a pretty good answer for that last one," I said, looking at Mark.

"Let's hear it," said David.

"It starts with the three laws of robotics."

"Three laws of robotics?" said Renee, as though I had asked for a roadmap of Mars.

"Wait a minute," said Lucas. "I remember . . . something from the movie . . . *I, Robot. I, Robot,* that's the one."

"I'd forgotten that, but you're right, they were listed at the start of that film," I said.

"A robot may . . ." Lucas had stood up, eyes closed and head down, pounding his right fist into his left palm, slowly, straining for the words, which suddenly started tumbling out of his mouth, "not injure a human being or, through inaction, allow a human being to come to harm!" He finished on a rising note to scattered applause.

"Impressive," I said. "Do you know the other two?"

"Once you get the first one, the others are easy," Lucas said, warming to the task. "Rule two: A robot must obey all commands except those that violate the first law. And Rule 3 states that a robot must protect his own survival, except when that would conflict with the first rules."

"Isaac Asimov, a scientist and author of science fiction, came up with those rules many years ago," I said. "He became skeptical of popular stories of his time, which commonly portrayed robots as sinister devices, raging out of control, attacking their human inventors."

"Like the Frankenstein story," Mark said.

"Exactly," I agreed.

· ☕ ·

None of this made sense to Asimov. He reasoned that human beings equip all tools with safety devices. We put a haft on a knife to protect our fingers; we equip guns with safety catches to prevent them from firing accidentally; and we use fuses or circuit breakers to prevent electrical wiring from overloading. From this, it seemed a reasonable conclusion that any society technologically advanced enough to build something as sophisticated as a robot would equip those robots with appropriate safety measures. Since we program robots like a computer, Asimov proposed that these safety devices would become laws, fundamental instructions implanted in the robot's brain, so that the robot could not disobey.

· ☕ ·

"And that relates to Mark's question how?" said Renee.

"No, I see it," said Mark. "He's sharpening the point. If Isaac Asimov could think of rules to make robots behave safely, why didn't God make the devil at least as safe as Asimov's robots and keep him from 'harming [other created] being[s]'?"

"And while He was at it, why didn't God make *us* safe, immune to temptation?" I asked.

"OK. We see the problem," said David, "but I'm not hearing any answers. Why didn't God make the devil, and us, at least as safe as Asimov's robots?"

"Because, although robots can theoretically be made safe, they cannot be free," I said.

. ☕ .

The very word *robot* comes from the Czech word *robota*, meaning "forced work or compulsory service," or *robotnik*, meaning "slave." In medieval times, the law of serfdom bound peasants to the land. This forced them to stay and farm, even if the lord of the manor exacted taxes that confiscated most of what they produced. Should they attempt to leave, they could be severely punished or even killed.

Anyone in forced labor—serfs, slaves, or prisoners—naturally reacts to their servitude by doing as little as possible, out of resentment sabotaging their masters in dozens of little ways, cooperating only under coercion, never willingly. Psychologists have a term for such minimal, grudging cooperation. They call it passive aggression.

. ☕ .

"Passive aggressive!" said Renee. "That's nasty. We studied passive aggressive behavior in freshman psych. I hate it when people act that way!"

"It's a natural reaction. We all feel that way. And we especially hate it," I said, "when someone we love acts that way. Teenagers often do it just to annoy their parents—of course, none of you ever feigned ignorance or helplessness in order to get out of doing something—did you?" No one rushed to answer that question, but the exchange of rueful grins said it all.

"Whenever we encounter this robotic behavior, we dislike it intensely. Would you want your boyfriend or girlfriend or spouse to love you robotically? Of course not," I said. "Why would any supreme being worthy of respect want that sort of relationship with us, any more than we want it from our loved ones? Obviously, he wouldn't."

"So God didn't make the creature we now call the devil as a robot, without a will of his own. God gave him freedom. And the devil used his freedom to rebel against his Maker, something no mere robot could do."

"Wait a minute—where do you get the idea that the devil rebelled?" said David.

"Oh, pretty much from everywhere," I said.

"Huh?" a collective expression of disbelief filled the air.

"It's one of a half-dozen or so universal ideas about reality. Sometimes we call these ideas 'myths,' " I said.

"I thought a myth was something imaginary, something made up, not real," said Mark, "like a fable or a fairy tale."

"Well, yes and no. Myths are the stories we use to explain reality that includes the spiritual and the supernatural," I said. "Science can't tell us anything about good and evil or if a devil exists. So, how the devil came to be has to be explained by something other than science, something that takes into account the spiritual and the supernatural."

"And that's how a myth functions?" said Mark.

"Can you give us an example?" asked Caroline. "One of my teachers said the idea of a personal devil is just an 'artifact of Judeo-Christian culture.' He says it's all pretty much capitalist propaganda."

"Well, when it comes to the idea that the devil is a being that rebelled against the authority of God, there are many myths—narratives that explain that process."

· 🜹 ·

Throughout history, people of every culture have struggled with the problem of the goodness of life and the presence of evil. They see much in life and in the world around them that is joyful and good and desirable. But they also see disease, decay, and death. For them, as for us, evil and death don't just seem inconvenient, but they violate our very sense of what ought to exist. Interestingly, many of these cultures explain the beginning and existence of evil in very similar ways.

Norse mythology speaks of the great and good Odin, ruler of Valhalla, the Norse paradise. But among the residents of that happy place we find Loki, the god of mischief, always at odds with Odin, disrupting the harmony of Valhalla. In Aztec lore, Tezcatlipoca envied and fought with the benevolent Quetzalcoatl. In Greek mythology, the Titans rebelled against Uranus.

Many cultures picture the cosmos as an originally happy place until envy infected one of the inhabitants, who then began plotting against the great ruler of the universe. The Hebrew Bible agrees that the evil one started out good but then chose the path of deception, betrayal, and rebellion.

. ☕ .

"With so many diverse cultures repeating the same basic story, it seems likely to me that the story must be based on some deep truth," I said.

"I can see that," said Mark.

"I'm wondering how you 'just happen' to know so much about these other cultures and their myths?" said David. "Doesn't seem natural to me."

"You're quite right. I don't 'just happen' to know these things. I've studied these same questions for many years. Over time, you pick up a lot of interesting details. Some of them stick."

"These questions," David asked, "how did you know what questions we'd ask?"

"Sooner or later, everybody asks these questions," I said. "I'm just a little older, so I asked them sooner and have been seeking answers longer."

"Well, OK," said David.

"Wait a minute, that still doesn't solve the problem," Caroline said. "If God didn't create the devil, does that mean the devil somehow created himself?"

"No. None of the stories picture the devil as a new kind of being but more like what we might call a 'failed being,' a creature ravaged and deformed by his own anger and bitterness into something less—not more—than he might have been."

"Like Gollum!" said Lucas. "Just like the ring in *The Lord of the Rings* transformed Gollum from a normal Hobbit to a ghastly parody of one, so you're saying the devil's rebellion transformed him from a once beautiful being into the horrible thing we think of as Satan."

"So, the devil didn't create himself, but he did sort of create evil," Caroline gave voice to her thoughts. "Would that be right?"

"I wouldn't say that, no. He didn't create anything," I answered.

"So, where did sin and evil come from?" Caroline asked.

"From the same place as darkness, cold, and death."

· ☕ ·

A number of years ago I visited a newspaper photo lab. Above the darkroom door, a red light indicated when the lights inside the darkroom were turned off. Just below this red light, a sign explained: "This is a darkroom. Please don't open this door when the red light is on. If you do, all the dark will leak out." We laugh, because we realize the problem isn't keeping the darkness in but keeping the light out. Darkness is the absence of light. We can tell because the presence of the tiniest spark dispels darkness. A single small candle can illuminate a large room. Strike a match at night, and it can be seen for miles.

We talked about this a couple of weeks ago, I think. You know, that darkness, cold, and sin actually don't exist except as negatives, as shadows. We can purchase a light bulb to brighten a dark place but not a "dark bulb" to dim a bright one. We can only block out the light. We can light a fire and warm a cold place, but even when we refrigerate something, we do so by moving heat.

· ☕ ·

"So, you're saying that evil does not exist?" said Caroline.

"In a way. Only goodness exists; evil describes the absence of goodness," I agreed.

"But what is goodness, then?" asked Caroline, becoming frustrated. "I mean, if a shadow indicates the absence of light, then evil indicates the absence of—what?"

"I know what my parents would say," volunteered David, making a face. "They'd say 'obedience.' Are you going to tell us that?"

"Well, it depends upon your perspective, as a Christian—" I began.

"My parents say they're Christians. I know lots of Christians who would say obedience."

"I do too. But that wouldn't convince me," I said.

"OK," said Caroline, "what would you say it is?"

"Wait. First I'd like to hear why it's *not* obedience," said David, to background sounds of agreement.

"Well, robots obey. They do exactly what we tell them, nothing more and nothing less. But since a robot cannot make any other choice, it cannot be good or bad." I saw puzzled looks, so I elaborated. "A robot either works as designed and instructed or it doesn't work, but to speak of an 'evil robot' really means to speak of a robot used by some human being for evil purposes. So, it's the person commanding the robot that's responsible for the evil."

"Whoa!" said David. "I thought Christianity was all about perfect obedience."

"Well, that's not the way I understand it. I don't think the God I believe in wants robots for children any more than I do. Consequently, I don't think that evil can be defined as the absence of obedience. But that's another discussion," I said.

"How about faith?" said Lucas. "Is evil the absence of faith?"

"Depending on how you use the word, I'd say yes," I replied.

"What do you mean, 'how you use it'?"

"Faith has several meanings," Mark said. "It can mean 'body of belief,' it can mean 'religion'—as in 'what faith do you belong to?' "

"How would you use it, then?" Lucas turned back to me.

"I would use it in the sense of trust," I said. "I understand Christianity to be about learning to trust God, and in the process becoming more trustworthy myself.

"Faith can mean simple belief," I explained, "agreeing or assenting to certain statements, but a person could agree with something and still lie about it. But most of us are looking for people whose actions match their stated beliefs. We can trust such people. I believe God is looking for the same thing: people who trust Him."

"I remember what you told Jim—about trust," said Renee. "About how trust forms the substance of any healthy, living, loving relationship." She gave David a warm look.

"That's my experience," I said. "And distrust, doubt in the sense of disbelief, and suspicion are just the shadows that remain when trust departs.

"I think all those great myths are telling the same real story. Lucifer, Loki—whatever you want to call him—became the devil when he ceased to trust his Maker, when he doubted His goodwill, and became suspicious of His government."

"So, let me get this straight," said Caroline. "When we see distrust, doubt, and suspicion, that's an emptiness we call evil."

"Doesn't it feel that way, when someone betrays your trust?" I asked. "Don't you feel so empty? I do." Everyone looked pretty serious.

Eventually Mark broke the silence. "So that emptiness always existed. The devil didn't invent emptiness; he was just the first to . . . to . . ." he paused, searching for the word, "to choose emptiness!" He looked at me. I just nodded.

"He didn't invent death . . . " I said, waiting.

"He just abandoned life," said Caroline.

"He did not invent darkness," Mark began reciting, "he rejected light. He did not invent cold, he distanced himself from warmth. Wow!"

"All the old tales agree," I said. "God created a powerful being who rejected His greatness and embraced nothingness. The devil didn't create nothing; he just made it appear desirable. For him, and for some others, it has become their heart's desire. Eventually, they will get what they want."

Outside, the sun had long since set, leaving the city in darkness.

The FAQs of Life

• • • • •

I brought my laptop to the café, even though I knew it was a mistake. Rose had installed wi-fi at Grounds for Belief. With three writing deadlines imminent, I had to choose between working at the café and not going at all. I didn't want to miss the opportunity to meet with friends, but I recognized that I ran a couple of risks in taking my work there, one risk being that I might not get much work done.

When Mark walked in and came over to my table, although I tried to look studious, he quickly deduced my true status. "Trouble hooking up with the Internet?" he said nonchalantly. Now, it's true that in my teenage years a laptop meant one of those magic eraser slates you could use over and over, but it's *not* true that when I was a young child, a laptop consisted of a clay tablet and a sharpened quill. No one ever used a quill for writing on a clay tablet in those days. We used sharpened reeds.

In any case, although I believe Mark continued to speak in English, I couldn't make out the dialect. Or rather, I could identify his cyberspeak—I just couldn't understand a thing he said. Eventually he realized he had lost me. It might have been my glazed eyes or my slack-jawed appearance. However he figured it out, he took pity on me. He got the connection up and running and then said, "If you need any more help, just go to their FAQs page."

"Facts? Why would I go there?" By this time, onlookers began exhibiting numerous stress behaviors—rolling eyes, grimacing, that sort of thing.

"No, not facts," Mark said. "F-a-q-s." He spelled it slowly, but I didn't recognize the word. "It's an acronym for 'Frequently Asked Questions.' FAQs." A few more keystrokes and up came the proper page titled "FAQS."

"I wish life had a FAQs page," said David.

"You look a little down," I said. "Is there a problem?"

"Well, I'm having trouble in one of my night classes. Makes me wonder if I've chosen the right occupation. And then there's Jim," he said.

"I remember Jim," I said. "How's he doing? Haven't seen him for a while."

"Well, that's just it. Remember I told you his wife had left him while he was overseas?" David said. I nodded. "Well, he's having trouble finding a job. And to make matters worse, his mom isn't well. She's been hospitalized."

"Oh, I'm sorry to hear that," I said. "Do they know what the problem is?"

"No," David said, "they don't. They're just giving her tests for now." We sat, not speaking for a moment or two. "Jim asks me for advice, and I don't even know what I'm doing, much less what to tell him. I just feel—I don't know—like I'm drifting. In the military, everything was decided for you. You might not like it, but you knew your future was planned. Now it's different. For both of us. Jim and me.

"You'd think," he said, "with all the information available on the Net, you could find out anything you need to."

"I know what you mean," I said. "It occurred to me that, with all the gigabytes of data at our fingertips, our Silicon Testament, surely we could find the answers to our most important questions."

"Seems like it," David agreed.

"Why not try it?" Mark said. "Go ego surfing."

"Ego surfing?" My voice was part of a chorus of curiosity.

"Sure," Lucas said. "That's where you type your own name into a search engine and see what shows up. Ego surfing."

· ☕ ·

So I tried it. I entered my name into one of the most popular search engines (which shall remain "Google" nameless). It was like looking into a funhouse mirror; an image of myself, along with some others who share my name, distorted, truncated; but nothing new. Just so much data, good and not so good. But meaning? Answers to the great questions of my existence—Who am I? Why am I here? Where am I going? No. Not even close.

As we looked through the various entries, my thoughts raced. I realized that something strange has taken place. We have more affluence, more ease, more leisure, more time to reflect, and more information. We have access, directly through travel and indirectly via the Internet and modern communications, to more of the world than ever before. Yet, searching this torrent of information leaves us more alienated rather than less.

That's because many of the very people who can explain how many hours of design and testing it took to produce these devices and applications will tell you that human beings evolved from nothing. According to this view of things, computers and software must be carefully thought out, while the infinitely more complex designer of the computer, a human person, "just happened."

No wonder we feel alienated. In a world increasingly dominated by intricately designed and fabricated devices, created for the purpose of making our lives better, only we human beings have no meaning—for what does an accident mean? No matter how long the chain of accidents, they still just happened, lacking purpose and devoid of meaning.

· ☕ ·

"Garbage in, garbage out," said David, rousing me from my reverie. Did he have perhaps a twinkle in his eye?

"Ow-w-w-w!" This from Renee. "That's harsh."

"No, he's right," I said. "That's the problem with the Internet, with computers in general. They only retrieve and process what we give them. If what we put into the system makes no sense, then what comes out won't either."

"So, the only answers we get out are the ones we—or someone—has put in," Mark said.

"Most of the people who invented all this are still alive," said Lucas.

"Who are you talking about?" asked David.

"Well, there's Sir Tim Berners-Lee, who invented the World Wide Web," Lucas said. He thought for a minute and then added, "I think he teaches at Massachusetts Institute of Technology."

"What about Bill Gates?" Renee asked, quite pleased with herself.

"Of course," said Mark. "Founder of Microsoft, richest man in the world, and a knight, to boot."

"I didn't know he was a knight," said Renee. "You mean Sir Bill Gates?"

"I don't know what they call him, but Queen Elizabeth II knighted him," said Mark.

"Maybe we could find a way to contact those guys," said David, not seeming optimistic.

"Well, they know a good deal about technology, but they don't have any better grasp of the future of a single individual than you and I do," I said. "They can explain the design and purpose of technology, but that doesn't mean they can help us to find meaning in our own lives."

"Wait a minute," said David. "They make manuals and diagrams that explain the functions of the various things they make, like chips, computers, and software. There ought to be a manual for me, and for Jim too. What about that intelligent designer, wouldn't he supply a manual, some sort of instruction book for us?"

"Maybe a Help function—some way of dealing with life's Frequently Asked Questions," Mark added.

"You mean the FAQs of life?" A grinning Lucas met with groans all around. "No, seriously, I mean, wouldn't your Intelligent Designer at least provide the minimal level of support we get from corporations like Microsoft or Dell?"

"Sure," I said. "I believe He did, in the collection of writings called the Bible."

"I knew you were going to say that," said David, clearly annoyed. "I just knew it!"

"I see that puts you off a bit. I don't blame you," I said. "Some people make the most extravagant claims for the Bible, and some really repulsive ideas have claimed support from the Bible."

"Well, how can you trust anything the Book says, if it's been so misused?" David said. "Makes me wonder if it's being misused, or maybe that's just what comes from reading that old Book."

"I understand why you would feel that way," I said. "But you realize, don't you, that all those outlandish claims, and some people's attempts to discredit the Bible with them, simply reveal how powerful the old Book must be."

"I'm not sure I follow you," David said.

"I never thought of that," Mark admitted, "but now I see it. Everyone naturally uses the most powerful tool we can find to help us achieve our goals or justify our actions. Since every genius and lunatic alike for centuries recognized the power of the Bible, they automatically used it to strengthen their case."

"That's right," I said. "We tend to forget that similar things—just as outlandish and monstrous—have been done in the name of science."

"I never heard of that," said David. "What are you talking about?"

"Nazism claimed its theories of racial purity sprang from the science of genetics," I said.

"That's right," said Renee. "I studied that last term in history class. And the communists used similar reasoning to claim science justified their atrocities."

"Still, that's only two. The Bible's been used for a lot more bad things than science," said David, with an air of "that settles that."

"Science hasn't been around nearly as long—" I began, only to have Mark take over.

"Yeah, science as an academic discipline is only a couple of centuries old, while parts of the Bible are more than three *thousand* years old. So, science hasn't provided as many opportunities for misuse," said Mark.

"But the body count from the abuse of science has already overtaken that of the misuse of religion," I said. "That doesn't make science either a fraud or inherently dangerous. It's simply a recognition of the power of science as an idea."

"So you're saying that just because people misuse the Bible for their own evil purposes, that doesn't discredit the Bible any more than abuses of science discredit the proper use of science, is that it?" David asked. I nodded.

"Well, OK," David said. "But that still doesn't excuse the absurd claims made for the Bible, or the violence done in its name."

"Oh, I agree," I said. "But that brings us to the hammer problem."

The Hammer Problem

* * * * *

I give up," said Mark. "What on earth is the hammer problem?"

"Psychologist Carl Rogers said, 'When your only tool is a hammer, all the world looks like a nail,' " I explained. "For some people, the Bible is their only tool, their only hammer, and they beat on everything with it.

"But it's not just the Bible," I went on. "Maybe it's just me, but it seems like I run into more and more 'hammer people' all the time."

"Hammer people," David said without inflection.

"Sure, people who get consumed by an enthusiasm of some sort. That's their 'hammer,' and they want you to pound away at all your problems with it." I still didn't seem to be connecting, so I tried again. "For example, there are the fitness freaks. Tell them you feel blue, and they tell you to go jogging. When you express discouragement, they tell you to lift weights. Admit you're tired, and they may prescribe fifty push-ups as a remedy."

David opened his mouth in a wide "Oh-h-h-h-h" and began nodding slowly. "Gotcha!"

"They never ask whether your fatigue comes from too little rest or too much exertion; they just recommend more exercise," I said.

Caroline clamped a hand to her mouth and began giggling. Wide-eyed, she said, "I know someone just like that. But she's nice other-wise."

"Oh, of course. 'Hammer people' aren't bad people; they've just surrendered every other tool in their life skills toolbox and latched on to—in this case—the exercise hammer."

David said, "The ones that bug me are the 'pantry police.' " Nearly everyone joined in agreement.

"I know what you mean," I said. "My mother went through several phases of this. At one time, carrot juice became her cure-all, her dietary hammer to pound on every disease. Getting a cold? Drink some carrot juice. Feeling fatigued? Carrot juice. Got anemia? Drink carrot juice.

"It can be anything," I said. "The late Nobel laureate Linus Pauling (he won the prize for chemistry) prescribed vitamin C for nearly everything. Now, I have no doubt that exercise, carrot juice, and vitamin C provide many benefits. They may even be good for nearly everything that ails you. Still, when confronted with a broken leg or a gunshot wound or some other trauma, I'd be more interested in splints, scalpels, and sutures."

"But exercise really is good for you," said David, ever the marine.

"Of course it is, but you don't want to do jumping jacks on a broken leg!" I said.

"Granted," David replied.

"When we say that exercise or vitamin C or a hammer, for that matter, may not be useful in a given situation," said Mark, picking up the idea, "that doesn't mean they aren't useful in other circumstances."

"That's right," said Renee, who was something of an herbalist. "As a general matter, exercise provides many benefits to life and health. And vitamin C protects the body against many ailments."

"But just because someone discovers a very useful hammer," said David, catching on, "that doesn't turn every life situation into a nail."

"Even with good, useful things, you have to be aware of circumstances," I said. "For example, eighteenth-century British sailors led a strenuous life, and prescribing more exercise for them would have had no positive effects on the disease of scurvy. Yet a relatively small amount of vitamin C, found in lime juice, cured it entirely."

"Is that how they came to be called limeys?" asked Lucas. I nodded, and he said, "I always wondered about that."

"In the right situation, exercise, vitamin C, and hammers can produce seemingly miraculous results. I suppose carrot juice can, too, but," I said, making a face, "I've had all the carrot juice I ever want." This set Caroline to giggling again.

"But that's why people get so excited about them," said David, warming to the idea, "because they do work so well."

"In the right circumstances," I said.

· ☕ ·

Hammers, after all, have been around for thousands of years precisely because they are so useful. Driving nails, tapping boards or stones into position, driving chisels in wood or stone are all useful chores that hammers perform. It's only when we start applying them to tasks for which they are ill suited that problems come in. Driving a nail with a hammer works well. Driving a screw far less well. Reshaping glass with a hammer only destroys the glass, and an old proverb cautions us against using a hammer to kill a fly on our friend's nose.

This overuse, or misuse, of otherwise very useful tools becomes more difficult when we address more complex issues. Like how to live a good and happy life.

One of the most useful lifestyle hammers over the past two thousand years has been the Bible. Like the other hammers mentioned here, the Bible provides much useful guidance for life. Also, like the other hammers mentioned, it has sometimes been misused. Probably the most famous case involves the scientist Galileo.

· ☕ ·

Mark rolled his eyes. "Galileo," was all he said.

Puzzled, David said, "What about Galileo?"

I gestured to Mark, so he started in. "Galileo, following Copernicus, taught that the earth revolved around the sun, rather than the other way around."

"Well, doesn't it?" asked Caroline.

"That's just it. Church authorities," Mark said with a wink at me, "*hammered* Galileo with certain biblical passages that seemed to conflict with Galileo's view. For example, when Joshua 'commanded the sun to stand still,' some thought that indicated that the sun moved, rather than the earth."

"Well, wait a minute," said David. "Isn't that what it means?"

Mark gestured to me, so I said, "That story is about a battle. Joshua had his enemy on the run and asked God for more daylight to pursue them. As a marine, you can sympathize, right?" David nodded.

"Now, whatever you think about whether God actually made the daylight last longer, you'll have to admit that, at that point, Joshua—or any soldier—didn't care whether the earth revolved around the sun or whether they both did figure-of-eights through the galactic center. Even worse, he didn't have the time to listen to a lecture on celestial mechanics!"

"Gotcha. That story wasn't about the solar system at all," David said.

Mark picked up the discussion. "Galileo understood the difference very well, because he said that the Bible 'tells us how to go to heaven, not how the heavens go.' "

"They used the Bible as a hammer to silence Galileo," I said, "when they should have used a *telescope* to verify or refute his observations."

"I can see that," said David.

"So now we have this difficult situation . . ."

• ☕ •

Because the Bible has been misused, opponents argue against using it at all. They like to point to supposed errors and mistakes to invalidate it. That's like saying because my hammer doesn't work very well at removing screws, I shouldn't use it for anything.

To defend the Bible, some of its supporters have rushed to turn it into a universal tool. Some claim, for example, that the Bible contains no errors of any sort—scientific, historic, or any other kind. The Bible itself makes no such claims. The Bible writers weren't interested in genetics, electronics, celestial mechanics, geology, quantum theory, or a whole list of other topics.

• ☕ •

"Using the Bible to try to settle such questions," said Mark, "is just another attempt by some annoying people to turn the Bible into a universal hammer and to turn everything else into their nail."

"So, that brings us back to the question you asked, David," I continued. "I said the Bible contains answers to the fundamental FAQs of life. You wanted to know if you could really depend on a book that's been so badly misused. Well, let me ask you, is your car reliable?"

"My car? Sure. What are you getting at?" David seemed wary.

"Does it have any rust?"

"A little."

"Why are you asking these questions?" Caroline asked.

"Just bear with me a little. I think it will be clear eventually." Turning to David, I asked, "What about dents?" I asked. "Has it been misused or abused in traffic?"

"Hey! I drive that car sometimes," said Renee.

"Well, it's got a couple of dents. As for misuse, well, does driving above the speed limit count?" David smiled a little.

"So, it has been misused a little, and maybe abused some?"

He bobbed his head from side to side. "But how much does that matter," he countered, "as long as it gets me where I want to go?"

"Good point," I said. After a short pause, I asked, "Does it do your job for you—you know, perform your tasks at work?"

"Of course not."

"Will it fill your kitchen cupboards with food or give you medical care?" I probed.

"Of course not," David said, getting a little frustrated with me. "It's not intended to do those things. But it will get me to work, to the grocery store, and to the doctor's office."

"So, you have to put fuel in it and drive it to the locations where the things you need can be acquired?" I asked. "Is that right?"

"Yeah, but what's with these questions?" David asked.

"Well, the Bible is like your car. Is it absolutely true, historically and scientifically? Possibly not. But I don't go to it for mathematical equations or building plans. I do find, again and again, that it supplies worthwhile guidance in my life. It helps me make sense of life, informs my decisions, and brings me comfort in times of stress," I said. "It doesn't do everything for me, but what it's intended for, it does very well."

"Well maybe," David said. "I can see that. But I've still got problems with it. This all sounds nice, but doesn't this Bible you talk about tell of an angry, vengeful God?"

"Sorry to break this up, folks, but it's time to close," said Rose.

My laptop sat on the table, unused the whole evening. "I've got to get home and get some work done," I said. "I've got some heavy deadlines this week. But I'll make a deal with you," I said.

"What kind of deal?" asked David.

"Come back next week, after I meet my deadlines, and I'll tell you why I love an angry God."

"Did you say you love an angry God?" asked Caroline, clearly surprised.

"That's what I said. And I think you might agree with me." No one moved, so I said, "Next week."

Why I Love an Angry God

* * * * *

Writing deadlines shortened my week and caused me to push other tasks aside. Trying to catch up those neglected tasks made me late for Grounds for Belief. Rose, burdened with grocery bags, rushed into the back door just as soon as I pulled in to the unusually crowded parking lot. That seemed a bit odd to me, but I gave it little more thought as I hurried into the café, carrying my leather writing portfolio. Opening the door, I noticed two things: The café was full, standing room only, and as I entered, everyone stopped talking at once.

For some reason, as I stood with every eye on me, I immediately began wondering if perhaps I had left my fly open. In the corner of my eye, I saw David pull out a chair for me to sit in. Since it looked to be the only unoccupied chair in the establishment, and I couldn't think of anything else to do, I walked over and sat down on it, leaning my portfolio against a table leg. To break the tension, I said, "I suppose you're wondering why I called you all here tonight." The comment prompted a little laughter, but the crowd remained uneasy.

I leaned in toward David and said, "Somebody want to clue me in?"

Caroline spoke first. "I guess a lot of people want to hear why you love an angry God." A ripple of sound and motion in the crowd apparently affirmed what Caroline had said.

"Well, we could go around the circle and have each one introduce themselves," I said. "And when we're done, we can go get breakfast."

Some genuine chuckles came now, but the crowd still waited. For something.

"Some of us are here to protest the things you're saying." This from a man dressed in a business suit, whom I'd never seen before.

"Saying?" I responded. "Like what?"

"This business about loving an angry God," he said, "we don't like it a bit."

"And there are some other things," said another similarly dressed fellow on the other side of the room. "Like talk of myths from pagans and devil-worshipers. What are you filling these kids' heads with?"

"Well," I said, my face getting hot. "You know, I don't mind if you disagree with me. But when you show contempt for my friends here, that gets me a little annoyed."

"What do you mean," the first suit asked, "contempt for your friends?"

"When you ask what I'm filling their heads with, you're not treating them as adults," I said, my voice forceful but not yet loud. "Filling something indicates it's empty, and 'filling their heads' indicates not only that their heads are empty but assumes they're passively swallowing anything I say." I looked around the room. Several people, including both suits, had become upset. "That's . . . your . . . loss," I said, emphasizing each word. The room had grown quiet, or my voice loud, and somehow I found myself standing. So, I sat again and turned down the volume. "These 'kids,' as you call them, are thoughtful adults, both of which facts you seem to have missed. They're my friends, and they're far from the passive simpletons you portray them as."

My temper was cooling, or my good judgment returning, but in either case, I said, "Now, if you," I said, nodding in turn to each suit and to another fellow in a mock turtleneck and tweed jacket with large elbow patches, "want to discuss whatever my friends are interested in," and here I glanced around again, "respectfully, then feel free. Otherwise . . ." I left it hanging. "I'm going to have some hot chocolate," I said, going to the counter. And the whole café began to buzz. *Good*, I thought. *Maybe the fever broke.*

I sat down again, and the fellow in the mock turtleneck and tweed jacket with large leather elbow patches made his way through the crowd and came up to me. "I admire your honesty," he said, looking at me but addressing the crowd. That and his uninvited hand on my shoulder made me wary. "Most Christians don't admit they actually enjoy violence in the name of God. Of course, I'm an atheist and a pacifist myself," he said, "precisely because I find that vengeful God of yours repugnant." He paused, looking around the room, now putting his arm around my shoulders and leaning in even closer.

As he was doing this, Renee caught my eye and mouthed, "My philosophy professor." I gave her a slight nod. *That would explain his attire,* I thought, *"professor chic."* "I think you're morally confused," he said, rather too sweetly, "but at least you're honest about it. I like that attempt at integrity."

Now I realized that his unwelcome familiarity resulted because he was *complimenting* me, like giving a pat on the back to a young boy for his first failed efforts at bike riding. I gently removed his arm from around my shoulders and said, "Not on the first date." Caroline started giggling, and I saw several others who had overheard our exchange. My erstwhile confidant recoiled.

He seized the moment to commence his lecture. "People who love an angry God," he addressed the crowd, which quieted to hear him, "are all the same. Remember when the Twin Towers came down? People like Jerry Falwell, Pat Robertson, and this fellow," he said, touching my elbow once again, "as well as the Muslims in the Middle East, said it was the punishment of an angry God."

I licked my lips very slowly and then pursed them in an effort to remain silent.

"Such notions about God are not of recent vintage," he said. "All primitive cultures, primitive minds," he said, glancing back at me, "believe in an angry God. Whether Quetzalcoatl of the Aztecs, Kali of the Thugs, or Molech of the Canaanites, angry, bloodthirsty gods have been the norm, not the exception, in history. Ancient peoples struggled constantly to appease their angry deities." He paused theatrically. I could almost see the instruction, "Pause for effect," written at this point in his original lecture notes.

"Because of this, true believers feel free to emulate their 'God' and engage in violence with a clear conscience. Wars are stimulated by, and often fought in the name of, religion." He was warming to his task, certain he had us on the run. I looked around. He had begun to persuade some and irritate the rest. The two suits were looking at me accusingly.

"The horrible suicides and murders at Jonestown, Guyana, in 1978, and the continual threats and violence in the name of Allah testify that these ideas live today. Religion begets violence," he said. "Believe in God, and you become a warmonger." He turned and gave me a predatory smile, and made to get up.

Now I put my arm on his shoulder, just enough pressure to keep him from rising. "My new friend here," I said, indicating the professor, "like many others, reacts to all this by rejecting the existence of God. But he is mistaken about violence. And he just might be mistaken about God," I said, smiling. He looked back murderously, but his pose as pacifist trapped him. He responded with the false chuckle the occasion called for.

"Mistaken about violence," he said, with great gravity. "I think not."

"Oh, but you are," I said. "No matter how large the body count you attribute to abusive religion, the twentieth century demonstrated the unparalleled lethality of atheism. The great atheist ideologies, fascism and communism, systematically exterminated more human beings in one short century than all those killed in the name of religion in all the preceding millennia."

The professor tried to protest, but I had the floor and wasn't letting it go. "You made your case without interruption; now it's my turn," I said. The crowd rumbled agreement.

"During those ten deadly decades," I said, "millions of people died. Stalin intentionally starved and worked to death thirty million of his own people, and that came before the war with German fascists that exacted another twenty million Soviet dead. That doesn't even take into account the millions of American, British, and European dead."

"Those wars were thrust upon the socialist countries," the professor said.

"Perhaps," I said, "but everywhere godless systems ruled, men, women, children of all ages died in droves.

"No, my friends, the evils done in the name of God shrink before the atrocities committed in the name of godlessness. Even at its worst, the Spanish Inquisition did not approach, either in sheer cruelty or numbers, the horror of the Holocaust, the purges in Stalinist Russia, or the killing fields of Cambodia—to name only three of the purges perpetrated by atheist systems." My atheist friend had begun squirming, but I kept my hand anchoring him to his chair.

"All by itself," I said, "the twentieth century demonstrated that passionless, methodical killing machines like the Nazi death camps or the Soviet gulag are worse than an angry God. Even if my friend is right, and God doesn't exist, a nonexistent, false god beats atheism."

"How can that be?" asked David, and the crowd resonated with his curiosity.

"Even a false god at least offers a false hope," I explained, "a hope that not only sustains the believer but also *re*strains him. There are always some things a believer must avoid to achieve salvation. But no God," here I paused and looked at the atheist professor, "means no hope and no restraint—and that's a deadly mix."

I let go of the professor's shoulder. Seeing the crowd had turned against him, he marched to the door and left.

"That's all fine," said the first suit. "Atheism makes no sense to me either. But you've seriously mischaracterized the God I know." He smiled beatifically. "The God I know is not an Old Testament god of war," he said, "but the Prince of Peace. He does not punish or turn away anyone. He is full of mercy and kindness. Instead of judging his erring children, He forgives. And I must ask you," he said, "are you an ordained minister?"

"No," I said. "I am not."

"Well, I am," he said. "I admire your efforts, but you do more damage than you know. I believe you would benefit from a seminary education." Again he smiled, as if looking at a bright but slightly misbehaving child.

"Well, I thank you for your kind comments," I said, and I bowed my head slightly in his direction. "But I doubt that my seminary professors would agree with you. If it didn't work when I was twenty-five years younger, why would it work now?"

"I don't follow you," he said, his smile fading. "You said you weren't ordained."

"I'm not," I said. "But I did study in the Seminary, and I enjoyed it. But are you saying only people with your education can really understand God?" I asked.

"Well, no, I didn't mean to imply that," he said.

"I don't believe that either," I said. "In fact, my friends here ask really good questions, and they seem to understand things pretty well, to me."

"Well, anyone can understand the God I worship," he said.

"I can't," I said. "Although I can understand why you'd want to believe that."

"What could be better than my benevolent God?" he demanded.

"Nobody wants to believe in the rapacious gods of the ancients that the professor described. But finding atheism unacceptable, many take refuge in the sort of 'toothless' God you advocate. C. S. Lewis, the author of *The Chronicles of Narnia*, once described this god as a sort of elderly gentleman who 'liked to see the young people having a good time,' " I said, and that remark elicited a giggle from Caroline and grins from David and the other café regulars.

"The sort of indulgent god who likes to dispense blessings but never corrects or chastens his children," I said. "Above all, this god never gets angry."

"Well, I don't agree with all of your characterization, but in general, that's the God I worship," the pastor in the suit said.

"The problem is, no matter how appealing this god may appear at first," I went on, "he fails you in trial."

"How dare you!"

"What do you mean, he fails in trial?" asked Caroline.

"So long as things go relatively well for us," I said, "we like a god who demands little, winks at our 'small' indiscretions, who never corrects anyone, and generally stays out of the way.

"Do you really want a God who never gets angry?" I asked, and the suit started to speak. But I fixed him with my gaze and said, "Before you answer, do you want a God who can watch children starve or be murdered and not get angry? Do you want a God who witnesses the cruelty that human beings perpetrate on each other and just smiles? I don't. I don't think anybody really wants that.

"When disasters strike the earth, sweeping away thousands, when evil men visit pain and destruction on the innocent, when children starve and suffer terrible disease, your passive, indulgent god with his insipid smile seems to mock our suffering and pain.

"When evil strikes the innocent, we don't want to hear platitudes about love. We want action against the perpetrators; we want our toothless god to grow fangs. We don't want an indifferent god or a moronically pleasant god. When we see the innocent suffer from evil, we feel outrage." I looked at the group. Many were nodding. "We can't be comforted by a god who cares less than we do."

"But an angry God—" he started to object, but I was having none of it.

"The reason we fear and reject an angry God is that we know Him too little and ourselves too well," I said. "We know that, moved to anger, we retaliate. We see what harm our anger brings and know that it pales compared to the destructive potential of an almighty, angry deity."

"Ah, but we're all sinners. When we do evil, the power of your angry God will be turned on us," the pastor said. "What do you say about that?"

"There is our mistake. The gods of the Greeks and Romans, aside from their supernatural powers, were beings just like us. It's easy for us to think an angry God would act as we do," I said. "But the Bible depicts a God whose ways are infinitely above ours.

"When we get angry, we *strike out* to visit greater retribution and pain on the perpetrator. But the Bible tells of a God, who, when angered by the depredations of sin, *reached out* in compassion to eliminate the evil and end the suffering. Our anger seeks to end the evil by obliterating the doer. But the God of the Bible became one of us, to eradicate the evil deeds by *redeeming* the doers.

"Oh, yes, I love my angry God," I said, "because it is His love for me that makes Him angry at the evil that causes pain and death. Angry enough to do something to end them.

"It's up to you," I said, gesturing around the room. "Do you want a mechanical, unfeeling god, an almighty automaton absent of passion?" The question met with silence.

"Do you want a toothless, imbecilic god whose tepid smile betrays his lukewarm love?" Again only silence resulted.

"Does your God only get angry?" asked Caroline.

"Now there's a great question," I said. "No, in fact, the Bible describes God as supremely passionate. But these are pure passions," I explained. "Anger untainted by spite, joy unclouded by envy, sorrow free of self-pity, and compassion unsullied by condescension."

"Wow," said Renee, "that gives me chills."

"Now you've begun to see it," I said. "God is not *less* alive, *less* emotional, *less* passionate than we are but much, *much* more so. When we glimpse the divine passion, we discover what it means to be fully alive."

I sat down, drained, and the café regulars crowded around. The pastor in the suit huddled with a few others and then left, a cluster of unhappiness.

"Do you have any other examples of God's—well, God's passion?" asked Renee.

I chuckled. "Yes, I brought some with me," I said. "I did intend to talk about why I love an angry God tonight, I just didn't expect," and I made a sweeping motion with my arm, "such a formal setting.

"Here you go," I said, reaching into my leather portfolio. "I printed these out just before I came."

They read quietly, and finally David spoke. "I had no idea the Bible described God in such terms." I saw agreement in the group.

"Well, it's up to you. Nobody can tell you what you have to believe," I said. "But I can't believe in a God who cares less, who's less alive, than I am. That's why I love an angry God."

Here's what was on the sheet I shared at the end:

One description of God's anger:

"Therefore I will shake the heavens,
And the earth will move out of her place,
In the wrath of the LORD of hosts
And in the day of His fierce anger."
Isaiah 13:13, NKJV

Here's God as a grieving father:

"How can I give you up, Ephraim?
How can I hand you over, Israel? . . .
My heart churns within Me."
Hosea 11:8, NKJV

And God as a being of exultant joy:

"He will rejoice over you with gladness,
He will quiet you in His love,
He will rejoice over you with singing."
Zephaniah 3:17, NKJV

Death Support

• • • • •

Taking no chances the next week, I arrived early at the café. No extra cars populated the parking lot. I opened the door just a crack, peering around the edge to see what awaited. Although the place was nearly empty, I could hear a couple of voices in earnest discussion. At a table near the far wall, Caroline, Renee, and David—the source of the discussion—sat talking.

They seemed occupied, so I got a hot chocolate and a chocolate-chip cookie and moved toward another table. Just before I sat down, David called out, "Got a question." I joined them.

"I really like your passionate God idea," said David, and both Renee and Caroline nodded their agreement. "But I've—we've got a bit of a problem with that. See, I think your angry God fits in with eternal hell-fire, while . . ." He pointed to Renee, who took over.

"I just don't see how any God we could describe as loving could burn people in hell forever," she said.

Caroline added, "I just don't see how it's fair for someone—say, like the story of Cain and Abel? I don't see how it's fair for Cain to burn forever for one murder, while someone who kills a lot of innocent people burns forever too. Isn't God fair?"

"But sin deserves punishment, don't you think?" asked David. "God has to be just."

"I can see both points of view," said Renee. "I just can't decide between them."

By this time, most of the café regulars had filtered in: Mark, Lucas, and several others. The perpetual Scrabble game in the corner, interrupted the previous week, had started up again. The clatter of the wooden tiles in the trays punctuated the growing hum of human interaction.

"Hmmm," I said. "That's a tough one. Some people believe that God essentially will torture evil people forever. Not everyone agrees with that. A question like that, you have to be pretty convinced in your own mind."

"Are you convinced?" asked Caroline.

"Oh yes, I'd say so."

"Which way?" again Caroline, probing.

"Oh no. On a question like this one, you really have to be certain for yourself. How about if I tell you *how* I think about it?" I asked. "Then you can decide for yourselves." They just kept looking at me. So I started. . . .

. ☕ .

I knew a woman, once, who floated through time on an opiate cloud. Her body was alive, but her mind—I don't know. Her thoughts flowed and pooled, swirled and stagnated like murky water. In the fleeting moments when the waters cleared and her thoughts focused, she longed to die. In those moments of clarity, she shook her head, keening in almost animal misery, and clutched feebly at the intravenous lines that kept her alive. A flurry of small strokes nearly a decade before she died took her power of speech, along with most of her motor skills. The nurses and other strangers who cared for her clearly could see how much she yearned to end the perpetual pain, the interminable boredom, the intense loneliness.

The nurses would come, cooing or scolding, and check the needles and lines that enforced her solitary confinement, keeping her trapped within the maze of her own sorrowing consciousness. They knew that when the end came, it almost certainly would be with a whimper. But they could do nothing to end her suffering. Years earlier, someone had condemned her to this twilight existence.

. ☕ .

"Who would do such a thing?" said Renee. "That's just terrible. What kind of twisted person would do that?"

98

"That's just it," I said. "It wasn't a twisted person who hated her; it was her husband, who could not bear to see her die."

Expressions of shock reverberated through the group.

"Of course, he didn't mean for her to suffer," I said, "but when a stroke made her unable to eat for herself, he authorized a feeding tube to be inserted. Once he did that, he basically assured that so long as technology could keep her body functioning, she could not die."

"What was he thinking?" said Caroline.

"He had lost one wife, and he couldn't face losing another. Nothing could restore her health or relieve her sorrow. But that's not why he did it. He postponed her death so he wouldn't have to face up to his own fears."

"That was really selfish," said Renee.

"Looking back, it seems pretty selfish," I said, "but he did not mean her harm. At first she could recognize people and talk some, but the passing years eroded her functions. The effect was to isolate her from the external world." I paused and saw tears welling in the eyes of several. "Then, in a terrible irony, her husband died first. So, long after he would have suffered from her loss, she remained imprisoned in a body that could not heal and would not die."

"My stepfather—for it was my mother I'm describing . . ." Several gasps could be heard. "Yes, it was my own mother, who waited, helpless, as she grieved in her desolate twilight—my stepfather did a cruel thing, not because he wanted to harm her but because he wished to spare himself. I cannot find it in my heart to condemn him, despite the terrible consequences to my mother."

"Whoa, dude, that's harsh," said David. I just nodded.

"Yeah, he made a very human mistake," I said. "But if there is a God, He makes no mistakes. So, if He keeps people alive in an ever-burning hell, to torment them for eternity, He does so with full knowledge of the consequences. At least what we do to people, we intend as 'life support.' Burning people forever could only be termed 'death support.'

"No compassionate human being would do that, don't you agree?" I asked, to nods all around. "Do you think God could be less compassionate than His creatures?"

"No," said David, frowning and shaking his head. "It doesn't make any sense. It can't be true."

"Wait a minute," said Renee. "Aren't there passages in the Bible that speak about eternal fire and smoke ascending 'for ever and ever'?"

"Yes, there are. But words don't always mean just what you expect them to," I said.

"What do you mean by that?" asked David, his suspicions stirred.

"Well, in a different place or a different time, words mean different things," I said. "For example, one time while I was dining in Australia, I asked for a napkin. At first, it was met with deathly silence. Eventually, one of my dining companions handed me what I wanted and said, 'We call these serviettes.' Later, when I discovered that I had asked for what Americans call a diaper, I understood the awkward silence. So, words don't always mean what we expect them to.

"And there are other times when words don't mean what they literally say."

"You're going to have to give me an example," said David. "I don't follow that at all."

"We call them figures of speech," I said. "The technical term is *idiom*."

"Examples, please."

"OK. When I say 'Keep an eye out for the weather,' I never expect anyone to interpret that phrase literally. Not even my grandmother, who had a glass eye and could have complied without injury! Of course that phrase really means 'Be alert for adverse changes in the weather.' A literal interpretation would be painful *and* miss the actual meaning."

"OK, so what does that have to do with everlasting fire?" Renee asked. "Are you trying to say that's just a figure of speech?"

"Well, let's take a look," I said, rising and going to a small bookshelf in the corner. I knew Rose kept several Bibles there. I brought several back and placed them on the table. "A lot of people don't pay attention to the Bible's definition of everlasting fire."

"The Bible defines it?" asked David.

"See for yourself," I replied. "It's back here in a short little book called Jude." I showed them, and after a little paging back and forth, each found it in their own Bible. "It only has one short chapter, and in verse seven, speaking of Sodom and Gomorrah, it says, 'They serve as an example of those who suffer the punishment of eternal fire' [NIV]."

"OK," said David, "I see it, but I don't get it."

"Do you know where Sodom and Gomorrah were?" I asked.

Mark, who had been listening most of the evening, said, "Aren't they somewhere over by the Dead Sea?"

"That's what they tell us," I said. "Are those towns still on fire?"

"Oh," said Mark. "No. I see."

"Well, I don't," said Caroline.

"Sodom and Gomorrah suffered the punishment of 'eternal fire' according to that verse in Jude. But they're not still burning."

"Oh!" from Caroline.

"And it wasn't still burning when Jude wrote this," I said. "The Roman rulers would have noticed."

"So, 'eternal fire' must be a figure of speech," said Mark.

"Looks that way to me," I said. "I think it probably means 'a fire that cannot be put out.' But once it consumes its fuel, it goes out by itself, leaving only ashes behind.

"So, I don't think the Bible speaks of God torturing people forever," I said. "Besides, wouldn't a God who needs to torture people be something less, not more, than human? I mean, if we agree that no sane, caring human being would engage in such behavior, then how can we reconcile an eternally burning hell with a loving God? I can't."

The café had grown quiet. "I don't know about you, but whatever else 'heaven' means, to be a heaven worthy of the name, it certainly means no 'death support,' " I said. "No wretched sinners kept alive where we can see them suffer."

"OK. I can live with that," said David.

"Well, I don't know," said Caroline. "It just raises another problem for me. But if no one will suffer eternally, does that mean—I've heard some people claim it—that everyone will make heaven at last? Is that true?"

Ordinary
Monsters

• • • • •

Why not?" asked David. "If God is so good and so powerful, why not just save everybody in the end?"

"I like that," said Caroline. "Didn't you say that God isn't just waiting to zap us when we do wrong?" I had to agree with that.

"What about your stepfather?" Renee asked. "He made your mother suffer because of his own selfishness."

"Well, yes, he made a mistake," I said, "and it was for selfish reasons. But if everyone who made a mistake for selfish reasons had to be destroyed, the earth would be depopulated pretty quickly. Remember, forgiveness is at the very center of my beliefs," I reminded them. "If we can't forgive people for mistakes, well, we're going to be pretty miserable. Because we won't be able to forgive ourselves for our mistakes either."

"That settles it then," said Caroline. "Everyone will be saved in the end, because God will forgive them."

"I wish it were that easy," I said, "but there are some things even God can't do."

"Whoa! Wait a sec," said David. "Things God can't do?"

"He can't make us be happy," I said.

"Sure He can," David protested. "He created drugs, He could get us all high on serving Him."

"Physical euphoria isn't happiness," I said. "Or is it your experience that druggies are happy people?"

"Well, there is that," David admitted. "But, seriously, who wouldn't be happy to live forever?"

"Unfortunately, lots of people," I said. "Ordinary people. Monsters. Ordinary monsters."

"Ordinary monsters?" said David, "What does that mean?"

"Sure, let me tell you a story. It happened in late April nineteen forty-five."

· ☙ ·

Above their heads, a lethal rain of high-explosive shells tore away at the broken remnants of civilization. But Magda and her husband kept all of that far away, maintaining a semblance of normality for their six children. Even now, as troops stormed districts nearby, Magda sat, calmly combing her children's hair. Their grooming finished, nightgowns on, they sang a little song as they mounted the stairs to their bedrooms, where cups of special hot chocolate awaited them.

Did she stroke their hair as the sedative in the chocolate lulled them to sleep? Did she watch, or give each sleeping child a kiss, as the doctor administered the fatal injection? We don't know. We do know that with her maternal duties completed, she and her husband, Josef Goebbels, carried out the rest of their deadly plan. They walked out into the Chancellery garden, where, according to their plan, an SS orderly shot each of them in the back of the head.

· ☙ ·

"O-o-o-h. That's an awful story," said Renee. "I hate stories like that. Why'd you have to tell us that?"

"Because it's important to understand that there are some people who wouldn't be happy in heaven, who would go to unbelievable lengths to avoid heaven. You see," I went on, "just a few days before she murdered her own children, Magda Goebbels told Traudl Junge, Hitler's personal secretary, who survived till two thousand two to tell the story, that her children were 'too good' to live in a world that had rejected National Socialism."

"You're saying she would never be happy unless Hitler ran the universe?" asked Caroline.

"Do you doubt it?" I replied. "She and her husband not only had themselves killed; they murdered their six children so none of them would ever live in a world without Hitler."

"Well, but that was different," David said. "Those guys, those Nazis were nuts. They really were—what did you say?—monsters. They really were monsters."

"And you think such people would be rare at other times? In other circumstances?" I asked.

"Rare," said Renee. "Yes. There are always some, I suppose, but they're relatively rare."

"Monstrous times make for monstrous people," said Mark.

"Think so?" I asked. "Not too many years ago, a psychiatrist named M. Scott Peck wrote a book about evil. He titled it *The People of the Lie*."

"I've heard of him," said Mark. "Didn't he write *The Road Less Traveled*?"

"That's him," I said. "He practiced psychiatry in Connecticut into our century. He died in two thousand five. So, he didn't live in some exotic faraway place or distant time."

"I don't know," said Renee. "I have some friends in Connecticut—Kirk and Katy. It's pretty exotic."

Mark rolled his eyes at Renee and said, "So what about him? What does Scott Peck have to do with people like the Goebbelses?"

. ☕ .

In his book *The People of the Lie*, M. Scott Peck brings us face to face with everyday evil characters, *ordinary* monsters; real people whose thoughtless cruelty chills us because of its frightening ordinariness, its numbing normality. For example, Peck introduces us to "Bobby," brought to the psychiatrist because of his problems. Bobby's parents can't understand why their teenage son seems depressed. Well, sure, there is the fact of his older brother Stuart's suicide. That's been tough on everybody.

But his parents, hard-working people, doing the best they can, cannot understand why Bobby has to be so inconsiderate as to cause them more trouble. After all, his parents gave Bobby an expensive present for Christmas. A gun. Stuart's gun. *The* gun Stuart killed himself with.

These parents just cannot understand why Bobby didn't show more gratitude. And now, all his moping about caused them to miss work in order to bring him to the psychiatrist. So, they asked Dr. Peck to prescribe some medication to make Bobby less unhappy, less troublesome. When Dr. Peck suggested *they* might need some help, they became quite incensed.

· ☕ ·

"You've got to be kidding," said Caroline. "You're making that up."

"Check it out for yourself," I said, pointing. "I think Rose has a copy of *People of the Lie* in that bookcase over there."

"What frightens me about Peck's book," I said, "is how ordinary and common evil is. Not just in others but in myself. How easily I slip into using others as tools, viewing them as obstacles or blaming them for my own troubles. How quickly I lose empathy for hurting people on TV news, on the other side of the world, or just down the block."

"I suppose that's right," said Mark. "Just in my lifetime, I remember ordinary people, former friends and neighbors committing horrific crimes against one another, in Bosnia, for example. I have relatives there."

"A friend of mine was actually in Rwanda during that awful time when so many were killed," said Erica.

"See, that's the problem," I explained. "The extraordinary monsters like Hitler and Stalin gain support for their hideous deeds by convincing ordinary people to blame others for their unhappiness. For Hitler it was the Jews. It's amazing, in a way. He convinced one of the most sophisticated and educated populations in the world that all their troubles came from the Jews living among them."

"For Milosovic it was the Croats and the Muslims," said Mark. "These extraordinary monsters, as you call them, do indeed turn ordinary citizens into ordinary monsters. Soon monstrous behavior becomes normal."

"It often happens that way," I said. "But you don't have to be part of some great social or political movement to become an ordinary monster. Some individuals simply decide that everyone else's existence is less important than their own, and begin to act that way. These little tyrants come to hate everyone who frustrates their desires. They don't actually kill the objects of their spite, as Hitler did, but they would if they could. And they vent their fiery anger on all within range, as often as they please.

"Or like Bobby's parents, they simply see everyone else as moving furniture, to be used, abused, or neglected—ultimately frozen to death by the icy hatred called indifference."

"You're right," said David, his voice catching. "Sometimes the cruelest people are people in the same church. Even the same home." Renee put a hand on his shoulder as he covered his eyes.

"We all know these little tyrants of fire and ice, don't we?" I asked, and saw no disagreement in the now very quiet room. "What can God do with them?

"I'd like to agree with those who say things like, 'We all worship the same God,' and that 'we're all going to heaven by different roads,' " I went on. "Well, maybe. But how about the Nazis and the Jews? Can you imagine a place where both ardent Nazis and devout Jews were forced to live together, forever? Could either of them call that place heaven? Or would it seem more like hell? Or how about the Tutsis and the Hutus of Rwanda? The Bosnians and the Serbs? The Ku Klux Klan and African Americans?

"I wish it weren't so," I admitted, shaking my head, "but history and my own personal experience both tell me there are certain people who are only happy when picking on someone else; that there are some predatory human beings who cannot be happy without their prey. But the people being preyed upon cannot have peace so long as the predators exist."

"Why doesn't God just perform a miracle and change the predators?" asked a very sobered Caroline.

"He will, if they will let Him," I said.

"But if they don't want to be changed?" asked Mark.

"Anybody remember the movie *The Stepford Wives*?" I asked.

"Oh yeah," said Lucas. "That's the one where difficult real human wives were replaced with always compliant, cheery, perky android wives?"

"I didn't like that one," said Caroline. "It was creepy."

"That's the whole point," I agreed. "So, would you want God to change Hitler, and all the other monstrous people, into smiling 'Stepford Christians'? And how would you feel toward God? Would you want to please Him because you loved Him or because you didn't want to be turned into a grinning robot yourself?"

"It's not any better, really," said Mark.

"What's not?" asked Lucas.

"It's no better to say, 'If you don't love me, I'll turn you into a mindless robot that appears to love me' than to say 'If you don't love me, I'll torment you forever,' " Mark explained. "They're both torture, really, just different kinds."

"So, if you were God, what would you do to solve the problem of evil people who don't want to change?" I asked. "He has essentially three choices: One, build a perfect world and receive as citizens all who want to live in such a society; two, remake the predators into 'Stepford Wives'; or three, mercifully put the predators out of their misery.

"God has promised to reestablish a world of peace and harmony," I said. "All the old religions agree on that. And God knows that like the Goebbelses facing a world without Hitler, these ordinary monsters would rather be dead. So, I think, in the end, God will reluctantly accept their choice."

I looked from one solemn face to another. No one offered an alternative.

The Corn God Myth

. . . . .

Lucas and Mark roped me into another game of Uno, which included David and Renee, and it actually looked like I might win one hand. Only two cards, a red "Reverse" and a "Wild" card, remained in my hand, and each player in turn played something red. All I had to do was play my red "Reverse" and wait till my turn came again—it looked like I had a chance. Just as it came to be my turn, Caroline sat down beside me.

"Last week," Caroline began, "you said something that stuck with me."

Gratified, I played my card and said, "Just one thing? I hope—"

Lucas, Mark, and Renee shouted, "Uno!" in unison.

Chagrined, I drew two cards. "I wish it had been 'Uno,' " I said to Caroline, now giggling behind her cupped hand. While she recovered, play went back to Lucas, a blue six on top of the pile. He daintily laid his last card on the pile, a blue "Skip," and began pointing at me and laughing. Mark tried to hide his amusement. David and Renee did not.

Mark began shuffling the cards again, but I held up both hands. "I think my pride has suffered enough tonight. I'll watch the next one."

Rose didn't have any raspberry turnovers that night, raspberry season having passed. But during the last Uno hand I had seen her put out some apricot strudel. I try to sit where I can see the pastry counter at all times; it's a survival skill. Rose flavors the apricot filling with almond and mint, making it even more irresistible. So, I went to the counter and got a piece, along with a large and very hot cup of chocolate.

Returning, I sat at the table next to the Uno game, where I could watch both the game and my strudel. I'm not pointing any fingers, but pastry has been known to mysteriously disappear from my plate. Caroline pulled her chair over.

"What you said," she began, "went something like this: 'If you were God, how would you solve the problem of evil people who don't want to change?' "

I just nodded. For me, fresh strudel is serious business, and I try to attend to business always.

"Well, I've been wondering," she said and paused. "How does God solve the problem of people—evil and otherwise—who *do* want to change?"

I pushed my food aside. Even strudel must yield to some questions. "Now *that's* a question all of humankind has been asking for thousands of years," I said. "And you know what? They all came up with the same answer."

"They did?" This came not from Caroline but from Mark, poised with an Uno card ready to be played. And echoed by Lucas and Renee.

"For thousands of years, people from virtually every culture on earth, from countless religions, were looking for the same thing—for the same *person*—to bring a solution for people who don't want to live in evil anymore."

"What answer, what person was that?" asked Mark. "I mean, they weren't all looking for *Jesus*, were they?"

"They were looking for the Corn God," I said.

"Who was that?" they said in unison.

· 🍵 ·

In the desert wastes and fertile valleys of the Nile, ancient Egyptians called him Osiris. In the coastal plains north of Israel, the Philistines called him first Dagon and later Baal. The Romans called him Saturn. In the land between the Tigris and Euphrates rivers, they knew him as Tammuz. In the high mountain basin where the Aztecs built the city of Tenochtitlan, he went by Cinteotl, or sometimes by his title, Xipe

Totec [SEE-peh TOW-tec]. The names and details varied to fit the language and worldview of each place, but the broad themes remained the same. Archeologists and anthropologists simply call him the Corn God.

· ☕ ·

"Whoa! Whoa! Whoa!" said David, silent until now. "How do you come up with all this Osiris and Saturn and Zippy Doo-Dah stuff?"

"Xipe Totec?"

"Whatever," said David. "Don't change the subject."

"Well, two reasons," I said. "One, I've been studying this idea for quite a while, and two, I wrote about it not long ago. Gave me a good excuse to brush up. Since then, it's just kind of stuck with me. Because I find it so interesting."

David didn't look convinced but lapsed back into silence.

"I've got a problem too," said Mark. "The ancient Egyptians didn't know anything about corn. Corn comes from the New World."

"That's true. I should have made that clearer," I admitted. "The word *corn* in Old English usage was a generic term, meaning 'cereal grain,' like wheat, oats, rye, and so on, and including what we call corn and the English call maize." Now Mark began nodding his understanding. "And anthropologists and historians are using that Old English generic meaning when they talk about the Corn God."

"And they discovered that essentially every ancient culture had a grain or 'corn' god, a god of death and rebirth, a god of sowing and reaping."

"I don't get it," said Caroline. "Why would they worship a god of grain or corn?"

"Because they didn't have soybeans?" Lucas asked, grinning. Caroline stuck out her tongue at him.

"Makes a lot of sense, really," said Mark. "In ancient times, people often suffered hunger, and famines killed more people than war. Under those circumstances, if something could prevent a famine, I'd be tempted to worship it too."

"Exactly," I agreed. "Disease follows famine, and death follows disease. And in the ancient world, famine meant a lack of grain, a lack of 'corn.'"

"I see," said Caroline. "That would make this Corn God pretty important."

"More than that," I said. "The Corn God ruled supreme because his followers, the farmers in an agricultural society, possessed a stability and prosperity that other cultures lacked. The hunter-gatherers were at the mercy of forces beyond their control; the nomadic herders could not remain in one place to build storehouses. The raiding horsemen of Genghis Khan could steal from the farmers, but the farmers always won in the long run, because despite drought and locusts, flood and warfare, farming provides the most reliable food supply. Besides, farming looks like magic."

"Magic," said David, clearly amused. "Farming looks like magic?"

"Sure. Look at it from their perspective. If you bury most things, they molder away. But if you bury a single kernel of grain, it springs back to life, a new life that returns many times its own weight in new ears of corn. Not only does this corn come back from its symbolic burial in death, it also provides a surplus to feed the family and enough to trade for gold or other goods."

"Corn, or most any grain, can be eaten whole, raw, roasted, or boiled," said Renee. "Grind it up, and you can make bread."

"Corn didn't just form the basis of their diet; it was the foundation of their commerce and sustained their very existence," said Mark.

"Now you're getting it," I said.

"No wonder they worshiped it," said Lucas. "The way they saw it, corn gave them life, physical survival, *and* material success. Looking at it that way, it would be surprising if they did not begin to worship it."

"It's also why the farmers, worshipers of the Corn God, always won out," I explained. "Three generations after Genghis Khan's horsemen terrorized Persia and the Caucasus, his descendants remained in authority, but by then, they, too, had become farmers. They, too, came to depend upon the Corn God.

"Of course, they recognized how much their lives depended upon the grain harvest, so they took every precaution to make sure that the harvest did not fail," I said.

"What do you mean by precautions?" asked Caroline. "Like applying fertilizer?" Everyone chuckled, Caroline being a farmer's daughter.

"Actually, they did, but they turned it into a ritual."

"Why a ritual?" Caroline asked.

"First, because the whole process seemed magical. Second, because it was so important, they wanted people to remember it. Like 'London Bridge' or 'Peas Porridge Hot,' they clothed the ritual in verse and action, so it stuck in the mind. It might be as simple as repeating a blessing and placing a fish in the hill with the seed."

"Like Squanto taught the Pilgrims?" said Renee.

"Uh huh," I agreed. "So, in the spring, the season of planting, the season of hope, the season of death and rebirth, they celebrated their festivals and made sacrifices to the Corn God. Oh, they worshiped him in gratitude for harvest in the autumn, but the great sacrifices came in the spring—"

"Because that was the time of greatest uncertainty," said Mark.

"But today we know a lot more about how corn grows," said David.

"Yes and no. We describe the agricultural process scientifically, but while it's true they did not know some of the things that we do today," I said, "it may also be true that we've forgotten some things they understood."

"What do you mean?" David asked.

"For example, we would say that a single kernel of corn contains the germ cells of the corn plant—the DNA. And when the correct conditions prevail—soil temperature, moisture, and so on—the seed germinates. Because we've named and described the process, we think we know what happens. But that doesn't mean that if we can link together the correct molecules of DNA and manufacture a seed, it will actually germinate."

"We can't? Why not?"

"You mean besides the technical problems?" I asked, and David nodded. "Because, despite all detailed information we have about the intricate steps of the germination process, when a seed germinates, something beyond the reach of science takes place."

"How can that be?" asked David.

"Remember, science can only tell us about nature—only about things we can measure," I reminded him. "When a seed germinates, well, life happens. And science still doesn't have a definition for life."

"It's a situation where the whole, the germinated seed, is more than just the sum of all its parts," said Mark. A pause followed as people digested those facts.

"If science can't tell us, then . . . ?" Caroline left it hanging.

"That's where myth comes in," I said.

"I remember that discussion," said Mark. "Several weeks ago. Myth attempts to tell of a reality greater than mere nature, a reality that includes the spiritual and the supernatural. That's what I remember, anyway."

"Yes, you expressed that clearly," I said. "And because it goes beyond nature, myth uses figurative or symbolic stories and language."

"I remember it vaguely," said Caroline, "but can you show us the difference between science and myth?"

"Well, science would describe something . . ." I held up my hand. "Just a second." Fortunately I had my leather writing portfolio with me, and I rummaged around in it for a few seconds. "Yes, here it is. Here's a scientific, in this case engineering, description of a human being."

I began reading. " 'A self-balancing, 28-jointed adapter-base biped, and electro-chemical reduction plant . . . thousands of hydraulic and pneumatic pumps, with motors attached; sixty-two thousand miles of capillaries, millions of warning signals, railroad and conveyor systems, crushers and cranes, and a universally distributed telephone system. . . .'

"You see, while each detail is correct," I commented, "when you add them up, you still don't have a human being, complete with hopes, aspirations, appetites, and quirks.

"By contrast, an old myth says God formed Adam out of the clay, breathed into him the breath of life, and man became a living soul," I said. "It doesn't give us either engineering or anatomical information, but it does tell us something about what it means to be human."

"You're right," said Caroline.

"Well, the Corn God myth has a similar purpose. It's trying to tell us something about death and rebirth, about sacrifice and harvest. What would you say if I told you the Bible also contains the Corn God myth?" As I said this, I walked over to the bookshelf and picked up a Bible.

"The Bible?" said Carolyn. "Seriously?"

"I can see that the story of Jesus' death and resurrection somewhat resembles what you're calling the Corn God myth," said Mark, "but unless you have something a little more specific, I think it's a stretch."

"Fair enough. How about this?" I said, and began reading. " ' "I tell you the truth, unless a kernel of wheat falls to the ground and dies, it remains only a single seed. But if it dies, it produces many seeds." ' "

"Let me see that," said David, so I handed the open Book to him.

"Right there," I said, pointing. "The Gospel of John, chapter twelve, verse twenty-four [NIV]."

First one and then another read the words and passed the Book along. "I wouldn't have believed it," said Renee, "if I hadn't read it for my-self."

"But the most spectacular example of the Corn God myth in the Bible occurred during the Last Supper," I said.

David looked a little puzzled, so Mark explained. "Remember that famous painting by Leonardo da Vinci depicting Jesus' last meal with His friends before His death?"

David nodded absently.

"At that meal, Jesus held up bread and said, 'This is My body, broken for you.' "

"I'm not following you," said David.

"What's bread made of?"

"Flour?" said David.

"And what is flour?" I asked.

"Ground-up grain," Renee prompted. "It's made of corn, in the Old English sense."

"Oh!" said David, blinking. "Cool!" Another blink. "Very cool!"

"Of course, He didn't mean the bread was literally His body," I explained.

"He meant it mythically," said Mark. "Wow!"

"It's almost like He's saying 'I am the Corn God.' My body will be broken for you as this bread is broken for you.

"Like the kernel of grain, His body will be buried. Like the kernel of grain, He will become alive again. And by eating the bread, you are tak-ing Him into your body, assimilating Him into yourself. He becomes part of you. So, His death becomes your death; His resurrection becomes your resurrection," I said.

"So, that's the real significance of the Communion meal, then?" said Caroline.

"It's beautiful," said Renee, "but I don't think many people would accept it. A lot of teachers, you know, like my philosophy professor, would say that all these legends simply arise out of prescientific superstitions. Or that they all, including the Bible story, came from oral traditions that stretch back into the mists of prehistory."

"And a lot of the Christians I know," said David, "would just say that this Corn God stuff is a corruption of the truth from the Bible."

"So what?" I said. "What if they're both *right*? Maybe these Corn God stories *do* come from ancient oral traditions. And maybe they *are* corruptions of a single truth. Maybe all the Corn God stories represent varying fragments, some of them distorted, but still fragments of a single promise made to human beings long ago. A promise that someone would come, would die, and be reborn in the spring of the year, and that his death and resurrection would signal the beginning of the end of death itself.

"And maybe, one time, the Corn God actually came to die, be buried, and rise again in new life. I believe the Bible says exactly that. And just as important, the Bible says that everyone who symbolically enters into the life and death of the Corn God would receive that same new kind of life. That's what I believe."

The End of Loneliness

• • • • •

"Will the café be open for Christmas?" asked David.

Outside, the late summer sun still shone bright. Only the first leaves had begun to turn, and the cicadas could be heard advertising their presence in the warm evening.

"I don't know," I said. "You would have to ask Rose. I don't even know what day of the week Christmas falls on this year."

Rose came in from the kitchen, wiping her hands on her apron. "Did I hear my name mentioned?" she asked.

"David here was asking if you're going to be open on Christmas. I said I didn't even know what day Christmas falls on this year."

"This year Christmas comes on Tuesday, and I'm taking it off," Rose said, nodding to emphasize her words. "In fact, I'll be with my family in Missouri that whole week. Holly's going with me, and we're going to have a real holiday." Finished with her declaration, she returned to the kitchen.

"Good for you," I called after her.

One by one the regulars filtered in, and David asked them about their holiday plans. It seemed that this particular year, everyone planned to be somewhere else.

"Why do you ask?" Mark wanted to know.

"Remember Jim?" asked David, and most of us nodded. "He's having a rough time right now."

116

"I remember his mother was ill," said Erica. "How is she doing?"

"That's just it. The doctors only give her a couple of months. She probably won't make it until Christmas. I've been planning for two years to spend this Christmas with my family in Oregon. This will be their first chance to meet Renee, so I really have to go. Otherwise, Jim could spend Christmas with me," David said. "He doesn't have a lot of friends around here, and I'm just concerned that being alone at Christmas will be rough for him."

"Alone at Christmas," I said, grimacing and shaking my head slowly.

"That's so sad," said Caroline. "I can't think of anything sadder."

"No, it's hard to imagine pouring more melancholy into fewer words," I agreed. "I mean, you can imagine phrases that might produce more fear or grief or outrage. But for simple sadness, however, it's hard to match the feeling of being alone, separated from family and friends, at Christmas."

"That's really true," said Mark. "More than any other time of the year, at Christmas we long to be with family. I wonder why that is?"

"Well, actually, it's deeply imbedded in the nature of Christmas itself," I said.

"I don't believe it," said Erica. "You're not going to tell us there's some deep meaning to being lonely at Christmas, are you?"

"You tell me," I said. "Do you feel a deep need to be with family at Christmas?"

"Well," Erica said, reflecting. "I suppose I do. Sure."

"You mean Christmas isn't just about getting presents?" this from Lucas, and Erica made as if to hit him.

"I don't know which one of you is worse," Erica said. "See," she said, turning to me. "For some people it's more about gifts."

"Well, certainly we associate gift giving with Christmas too," I agreed. "But even the gift giving is more about sharing each other's company than anything else. Emerson said, 'The only gift is a portion of thyself.' I figured you knew that intuitively, because you are so thoughtful in your gifts."

"I guess you're right," Erica admitted. "For me, the perfect gift communicates the message that, even though we may be separated during most of the year, the other person is always in my thoughts."

"And it's that sense of *being present* in your thoughts that gives a gift its real value, would you agree? And without that sense of being present in your thoughts, a mere thing, no matter its cost, just doesn't carry the same value. Is that true too?" I asked. As I spoke she nodded silently, her eyes far away.

"In other words, *being present* matters more than *bringing presents*," I said.

"Yes." Erica's eyes now focused on me. "I have never said it that way, but that's what matters."

"I'd like to suggest to you that this idea of *being present* lies at the heart of Christmas," I said. "And it explains why so many suffer depression during what is otherwise a most joyful season."

"Well, if you're alone, like Jim may be," said David, "everyone else's happiness highlights your own lack of anywhere to go, of anyone to be with."

"Yeah," said Mark. "The Christmas holiday interrupts the busy schedule that keeps you from thinking about loneliness the rest of the year."

"And some people build up such high expectations anticipating the annual Christmas gathering," said Erica, "that nothing real could live up to it."

"Then there are those who discover that being in physical proximity of family members only emphasizes their emotional separation," I said.

"It just seems so wrong—to be alone—even though you're with people," Erica said. "Does that make any sense?"

"It makes excellent sense," I said. "That's what I've been trying to say. The reason for this sense of 'wrongness' arises from the meaning of Christmas itself."

"You're going to speak of myth again, aren't you," said Lucas.

"We can hardly speak at all of the true meaning of Christmas without speaking in myths. The power of myth hovers over Christmas like a luminous cloud," I said. "The mythical power of the central Christmas story is so potent that it continually spawns new myths."

"What do you mean, 'new myths'?" asked Mark.

"Santa Claus, for one. Frosty the Snowman, 'The Night Before Christmas,' Dickens's *A Christmas Carol*, the movie *It's a Wonderful Life*—"

"Oh . . . sure . . . now I get it," Mark said, waving his hand in surrender. "There are a lot of them, aren't there? Christmas *is* a myth that spawns other myths, and even some of *them* spawn further myths. Wow! Why is that?"

"Well, what is myth?" I asked.

"Myths are the stories we use to describe reality greater than nature, reality that includes the spiritual and supernatural," Mark said. "At least, that's the definition we've been using in our discussions."

"So, if we discover a particularly potent myth, what would that say about the underlying reality?" I asked.

"Oh," said Mark, who sat motionless, mouth still forming the word, eyes wide.

"What?" Erica looked at him in alarm, and then turned to me. "What's so 'Oh'?"

Mark looked at her and closed his mouth. "If we discover a myth of great power, then the underlying reality must be one of great power. In this case, enormous power."

"How do you know the power is . . . is 'enormous'?" asked Erica.

"Because it continually has exercised that power, without weakening, for more than two thousand years," I said, "and come this Christmas season, we may well see another manifestation of its power."

"Like what?" Erica asked.

"Oh, another movie based on *A Christmas Carol*, which itself derives from the Christmas story. Or another mythical Christmas song, like 'The Little Drummer Boy,' or even 'Rudolf, the Red-Nosed Reindeer,' " I said.

"Wait a minute," said Erica, "you're calling Rudolf a powerful myth?"

"An expression of a powerful myth, yes. The reason Rudolf remains popular after all these years is that it's an expression of a larger myth—about an individual who's rejected at first but who becomes the most important one of all," I said.

"The 'stone that the builders rejected,' " said Lucas, entranced, " 'has become the capstone.' I never made the connection."

"OK, OK, hold it!" demanded David. "What on earth is everyone talking about? Reindeer, capstones—*Christmas?* You gotta help me out here."

"The Christmas story derives its enormous power from the reality it describes," I said. "That reality is so deep and so powerful that it spawns other myths, and those other myths spawn yet others. And each is powerful because of the reality it describes."

"Yes, yes, we said that already," said David, "but how did we get to Rudolf?"

"Well, part of the Christmas story is that Christ was rejected by His own people, yet He was the Son of God. Now, that's a pretty big reality, wouldn't you say?" I asked.

"Big enough," said David.

"Well, Jesus embodies a reality so huge that we can barely understand it now," I said, "but, before He came, it was literally unimaginable. So the Old Testament prophets gave us pieces of the Grand Myth, so that we could recognize the reality when He came."

"I think I'm getting a headache," said Erica.

"And no wonder," I said. "It's still a lot to deal with, even after we know what happened."

"I just want to know about Rudolf," said David.

· ⛾ ·

One of the Old Testament prophets wrote about the building of Solomon's temple in Jerusalem, one of the Seven Wonders of the Ancient World. Solomon built the temple like a giant Lego set. Everything was cut to size offsite and then transported to the building site and put in place.

One day the quarry men sent a stone, but when it got to the building site, the masons rejected it. Later they discovered that their rejected stone was the capstone, the most important stone of all.

So, this became a proverb about rejection. "The stone the builders rejected has become the capstone." Centuries later, Jesus applied that proverb to Himself, that even though His people rejected Him, He would someday be of great importance to them. That little part of the Christmas myth not only remains with us but has spawned a whole bunch of smaller myths.

· ⛾ ·

"And when it comes to Rudolf," I explained, "he's like the capstone: originally rejected, later finding his true place."

"What others, besides Rudolf?" asked David.

"How about Cinderella or the Ugly Duckling?" I said. "They're all about being rejected at first and then exalted later."

David didn't make a sound, his eyes searching the distance.

"And that's like just one tiny beam of light compared to the whole story," said Mark.

"Well put. And the power of the reality at the center of the Christmas myth has protected it for all these centuries. In Christmas, many of the greatest myths, the greatest explanations of this broken reality we call life, come together. Like the Corn God myth, Christmas affirms that we were not meant to die. But Christmas goes beyond the Corn God myth, by assuring us that we were not meant to be alone, not meant to say good-bye. And Christmas reassures us that our fate matters to the Ruler of the universe."

"You said *many* myths. Give us another one," said David.

Erica grinned. "Habit-forming, aren't they?"

• ☕ •

Another great myth of ancient times revolves around the "ruler in disguise." In this myth, the ruler or ruler-to-be—a prince, king, ca-liph, or emperor—travels among his subjects in disguise (Shakespeare borrows this idea several times). The ruler does this so he can escape the isolation of the palace and discover what his subjects truly think and feel. Along the way, he encounters haughty nobles and officials, and at least some wise but impoverished souls. In the end, his true identity revealed, the ruler then rewards the humble and punishes the proud.

The Christmas story makes audacious claims, and it raises this myth to its highest possible level, for at Christmas, not just any garden variety ruler appears in humble attire. At Christmas, the Designer of all things appears as an infant, born in a barn.

• ☕ •

Renee had been silent all that time, but now she spoke. "My profes-sor, the one you met? He says that the Jesus of the Bible was a great moral teacher, even a 'counter-culture philosopher.' He says that

Christians don't even understand their own greatest Teacher. That all this talk about Jesus being the Son of God came afterward."

"But the record is quite clear. Jesus Himself claimed to be God," I told her. "Whether you accept His claim or not, He *did* make the claim. And to be honest, people who make such claims are usually either a sociopath or as crazy as a loon. 'Great Moral Teacher' and 'insane' don't go together very well."

"My teacher says we misunderstand those passages where we think He claimed to be God," Renee persisted.

"Of course it's possible, after two thousand years, that people could come to misunderstand what Jesus said and did," I admitted. "That's why the reaction of people in His day is so important. You see, the religious leaders of His day showed they clearly understood Jesus' claim to be God, because they took up stones to punish Him for blasphemy. And blasphemy in this case meant 'claiming to be God.' "

"Any chance He wasn't really human?" asked David.

"What does that mean?" asked Renee.

"I don't know, maybe He just looked human," David said. "I've heard maybe He was an alien."

"The people of Jesus' day didn't all believe His claim to be God, but they never questioned His humanity," I assured David. "This 'ruler in disguise' encountered life just as we do, in all its variety, all its fatigue, hunger, thirst, grief, anger, and love. His 'disguise' was so thorough that His envious neighbors used His humanness to put Him down: 'We've known Him since He was a kid; He's the carpenter's Son.' "

"Wait a minute," David said. "That's too much. How can He be *both* God *and* human? It's impossible."

"You're right. In scientific terms, it cannot happen. But remember, science deals only with the natural world. The Christmas story claims to be about a supernatural event," I reminded them. "And Jesus needed to be this mysterious, one-of-a-kind being, fully God and fully man."

"Why?" said David. "I mean, it really complicates the whole thing."

"Actually, it simplifies everything else," I said. "Because only in this way could He bridge the gulf distrust had placed between human beings and God. Being God, Jesus could explain what God really thinks about people. And being human, He can explain to God exactly how it feels to endure what we have to go through."

"The perfect ambassador between us and God," said Mark.

"But that's not all. The reality at the center of the Christmas myth is even greater," I said. "It's easy to think that Jesus was human for only the thirty-plus years He lived in Palestine. As though God just loaned us Jesus, only to take Christ away after He 'served His term' as a human being."

"Well, yeah," said Renee. "Isn't that enough?"

"Enough or not, the Bible claims that Jesus agreed to become a human being, knowing it would be a one-way trip, with no turning back— that Jesus became one of us forever," I said. "And that's why it seems so wrong to be lonely, and all the more so at Christmas."

"Tell us," said Erica.

"The event we celebrate at Christmas represents the end of loneliness," I said. "It's God's way of telling us that we were never meant to be alone."

"I see it. Because He's both God and Man, as long as He exists, the two are united in Him, in His very person," said Mark.

"And since He conquered death and can never die?" I asked.

Mark's voice grew quiet as he said, "God and humanity can never be separated again."

Unbreakable Hearts

* * * * *

David sat quietly for a long time. "Look," he finally said, "all this talk about myth and 'the end of loneliness' is good. It really is."

"It's not just good," said Renee, "it's wonderful."

"I think David has something important on his mind," I said.

And he nodded soberly.

"Let me guess," I said. "All this talk about powerful myths is fine, as far as it goes." I looked to see David nodding. "But what good is all that tomorrow morning, when you have to go to work?"

"Or when I visit my parents?" David said. "They claim to be Christians. For all I know, they believe in all this myth stuff you're talking about," he said.

I chuckled. "I kind of doubt that," I said.

"But they act just like everybody else," he said. "They talk about religion and the Bible, but if you cross them, they'll tear you apart." He looked me right in the eye and said, "So, what I need to know is, what good is—all this—Christianity stuff?"

"You don't really mean—" Renee started, but I held up my hand.

"I think he does mean *exactly* what he's saying," I said. "And I agree with it."

"You do?" both of them said at the same time.

"Absolutely," I said. "The last thing we need is more good advice, people telling us what we ought to do."

"It is?" said Renee.

David and I immediately replied, "It is!"

"Buddha gave good advice. Confucius gave good advice. For that matter, Socrates gave good advice. The problem that David's talking about doesn't arise from a lack of good advice," I said.

Renee, David, and now several others sat, stunned and silent. Then David spoke. "Mom and Dad have gone to church, read the Bible, even had family worship," he said. "It's not that they don't know what to do, it's that they don't *do* it."

"None of us is perfect," said Caroline.

"This isn't about perfect, Caroline," I said. "It isn't even about the fact that they don't do what they know how to do. Actually, none of us does. Not all the time."

"Then what's it about?" Caroline asked, and others echoed the sentiment.

"Two things, it seems to me."

"And they are?" Caroline prompted.

"First, the desire to be different. Lots of people really don't want to behave differently. They think they're just fine, and it's the rest of the universe that needs to change," I said.

"Yeah," said David. "I think that's the problem I see."

"We all feel that way, at least some of the time," I said. "We're all self-ish and want the rest of the world to accommodate our every whim. That's our natural condition."

"What's the other thing?" David asked. "You said there were two."

"Yes, well, it only gets more difficult," I said. "Did you ever try to change for the better and fail?"

"Well, sure," said David, to general agreement. "Hasn't everybody?"

"In other words, we have the desire but not the power? Does that sound right?" I asked.

"But that's even worse," said Renee. "Even if they want to, people can't change?"

"That's the problem that David has identified," I said. "Despite knowing all about the good advice of Socrates, Confucius, Buddha, and yes, Jesus, people either don't want to change, or they're unable to change."

Erica had been silent, but now she spoke, solemn and subdued. "Yes. I have an example," she said. Questioning glances made the rounds. "Aren't we forgetting someone?" she asked. Still no one spoke. I know I drew a blank. "What about Jim?"

"Ow-w!" I said, "There, you see, it's not just someone else's failure. It's ours. It's mine, personally."

"Jim being alone isn't your fault," David said.

"No, but this just highlights the problem everyone has," I said. "We want—*I* want to do something so Jim doesn't spend Christmas alone, but in the discussion, I forgot about him. Even though I had the desire, I lacked the power *even to remember* the problem, much less do something positive to help."

"Everybody forgets," said David. "That's not your fault."

"Yes," I said. "It's not my fault. But I don't want to see Jim after he spends Christmas alone and say, 'I forgot.' I want to become the kind of person who not only talks about caring for others; I want to actually care for them in practical ways. I want to be a blessing."

"So, does your religion have an answer?" asked David.

"The only answer I've found is a heart transplant," I said.

"Is this another myth?" asked David.

"Yes," I said and paused. "And no."

"Oh-h-h-h-h! I knew you were going to say that," said Caroline.

"Tell us about this mythical heart transplant," said David.

"OK," I said, "but first let me tell you about a real one. . . ."

· ☕ ·

I'll never forget the morning we got the telephone call: "They found a heart for Taylor." Eleven-year-old Taylor had been fading before our eyes as he waited on the transplant list. It's a strange feeling, watching someone you care for slowly drift toward death while waiting for a heart to "become available."

Diagnosed with a rare cancer at four years of age, Taylor had undergone years of surgery and chemotherapy. Eventually the doctors declared him cancer free, only to discover that the chemo had damaged his heart beyond repair. Half a century ago, that would have been a death sentence. But in the last couple of decades organ transplants, even heart transplants, have become commonplace. Doctors could give Taylor's parents, Bill and Jill, real hope. So, we greeted the news of an available heart with a mixture of hope and anxiety—and a real sense of solemnity.

· ☕ ·

"You mean you weren't ecstatic?" asked David. "Why?"

"I can guess," said Renee. "Because no matter how skilled the surgeons are, heart transplant surgery presents real risks. And they start by removing the living patient's heart."

"O-o-o-h-h!" said Caroline. "Just thinking about literally cutting out a living person's heart makes me shiver."

"Exactly. That's my point," I said. "No one would take a chance on such a procedure unless they were convinced that all the alternatives were worse. So, we naturally felt anxiety for Taylor, since he was about to undergo such a drastic procedure. And something else made us even more sober."

"Like what?" said David.

"We knew that a heart transplant offered the only real hope for him to enjoy something approaching a normal life," I said. "But hearts only become available when a donor dies."

"Oh," said David. "Right."

"The same event that gave us hope caused another family to grieve. Recognizing that someone had to die for an organ to become available tinges every such transplant celebration with sadness," I said. "Some organs for transplant—a kidney, part of a lung, for example—can come from a living donor. But a heart, a whole liver, or a pancreas must come from someone recently dead."

"Oddly enough, the Bible speaks of a heart transplant too," I said.

· ☕ ·

All of us are born with what you might call the congenital heart defect of sin. Sin and selfishness are those desires and tendencies that cause us to hurt others and result in personal grief, as well.

Like wounded animals, many of the hurtful things we do to others, and that cause us such grief, come out of a natural desire to avoid or lessen pain. But we do so in a way that makes matters worse: We harden our hearts to minimize pain, not realizing that a hard heart retains its hardened wounds. The wounds fester, seeping bitterness, and the surrounding flesh petrifies further. The acid of bitterness etches the record of grievances in the petrifying tissue and burns out life-giving love. These hardened wounds never go away, never heal. Eventually this process produces a heart of stone. And along the way, we grow less trusting and less friendly and become increasingly alone and desperately lonely. We lose both the desire and the ability to change for the better.

C. S. Lewis described the problem in *The Four Loves*, saying such a stony heart becomes "unbreakable—irredeemable." Yet, it's precisely this kind of heart that God offers to replace.

. ☕ .

"The Hebrew prophet Ezekiel depicts God saying ' "I will give them an undivided heart and put a new spirit in them; I will remove from them their heart of stone and give them a heart of flesh" ' [Ezekiel 11:19, NIV]," I said.

"That's more of that mythical language, isn't it," said Caroline, "describing something real but not scientific. Did I get that right?"

"Beautiful," I said.

"And it fits with the Corn God myth," said Mark. "Those who eat the bread, who enter into the Corn God myth, and thus accept Jesus' death and resurrection as their own will experience a 'change of heart.' " I pointed my finger directly at him and gave one big nod.

"And like any other transplant, this transplant promises a better life," I said, "not just a longer one. And like a modern medical transplant, our miraculous flesh-for-stone heart transplant does not come without serious cost."

"The donor had to die," said David.

"Like Jesus did," said Caroline. "He had to die so we could get a new heart."

The group sat quietly for a minute.

"There's more," I said.

Mark just shook his head. "You can't be serious."

"To be successful," I continued, "the new heart must supply what the old one could not. Remember what happened to our hearts?"

"They turned to stone," said Renee. "They became unbreakable."

"And here, the influence of myth intrudes powerfully yet again," I said.

"If you remember the plot of *The Passion of the Christ,* you know that Jesus died after only a few hours on the cross," I said. "Knowing that it usually took days for someone to die on the cross, a Roman soldier thrust a spear in Jesus' side, to be certain He had died."

"And . . ." said David.

"And then blood and water came out of the spear wound." Once again I paused.

"Which means what?" asked Caroline.

"Blood separates into red cells and plasma—what looks like blood and water—only when the heart ruptures—"

"You don't mean—" said Renee.

"Yes," I said. "He literally died of a broken heart. And that makes Him the perfect donor. Our old stony hearts became unbreakable, so the donor heart had to be breakable. And we know that it was because, in our case, the donor died of a broken heart."

"So, what does this have to do with the desire and the to power do right?" asked David.

"That's what the whole thing is talking about," I said. "According to the Bible, only Jesus had both the desire and the power to always do right."

"So, when we receive His heart, we get the power and desire to do right," said David. "I see that. But why doesn't it work for everyone?"

"Like your parents," I said.

"Like them."

"There's an old spiritual that says, 'Everybody talkin' 'bout heaven ain't goin' there,' " I said. "It's one thing to talk about Christianity, to learn the doctrines, but another thing to actually become a Christian."

"What do you mean?" asked David.

"Just like it's one thing to talk about surgery, but it's another one to go under the knife," I said. "Sadly, lots of people want you to *think* they've had this heart transplant. They try to act in ways that will convince you that they have really changed, but they're not willing to submit to the operation." I let that sink in.

"The good news is that, unlike medical transplants, we need not worry about the length of the waiting list and whether a suitable organ will be available in time. This spiritual, mythical, timeless offering is instantly available," I said. "But it's frightening just the same. Giving up control over your own life and asking God to take it over feels like dying, and not everyone is willing to take the risk."

"So, not everyone is willing to risk that final step," said David.

We all sat in silence for a while.

"If a person decided to take that final step, how would he go about it?" Again David was asking.

"Oh, there's no incantation, or magic words, no formula a person has to follow," I said. "All a person has to do is open his heart to God. Ask God to change his life and trust God to do it. This heart transplant is available today. Anyone can begin living a new life of increasing love and trust right away.

"There's one thing I should tell you about," I said. "This miraculous heart transplant promises a better, more vibrant life right now, but by itself, it does not eliminate death. Putting a new heart into an aging body only does so much. The rest of the body wears down, ceases to function. Death comes even for those with a pure heart. For thousands of years, God has given new hearts to those who sought after Him. Yet, death comes to them. As we noted earlier, God promises a life after death, but death still remains. For a while."

"For a while?" said Caroline. "What does that mean?"

"It means at least until next week," said Rose. "It's closing time."

Caroline started to protest, but Rose shooed us all toward the door. As we scurried to the exit, Erica said, "What are we going to do for Jim?"

"I may have a solution," I said, still moving, and added, "Next week!" as I hustled out the door. Rose is a sweet lady, but not to be trifled with. Especially at closing time.

Your Last Enemy

. . . . .

For several weeks, attendance was light at the café. Late summer vacations, followed by Labor Day, and then the opening weeks of school kept people busy all day and into the dark hours. Even the perpetual Scrabble game languished some weeks.

The days remained warm, but a chill haunted the evenings. Bright crimson leaves on the maple trees signaled the end of warm weather and the onset of the autumn. At the café, Rose would soon be serving hot spiced cider and fresh pumpkin pie. She might even bake one of her famous pumpkin cakes, the ones with cream-cheese frosting.

Perhaps others were entertaining similar thoughts, because a full parking lot signaled a busy night in the café as I pulled up. Sure enough, Mark and Lucas each were sitting before a large piece of pumpkin cake, a steaming cup of cider near at hand. I headed for the counter, hoping to secure for myself a piece of the pumpkin cake before it was all gone.

"Too late," said a voice behind me. I turned to see David and Renee sitting at their usual table near the far wall. Caroline sat nearby, with the curly headed guitarist fellow whom I had not seen for some weeks. Other familiar faces looked up at me expectantly.

A closer look revealed David gesturing to an untouched piece of pumpkin cake and a full cup of cider at their table, in front of an empty chair. Just the sort of offer I can rarely refuse. "Are you attempting bribery?" I asked, grinning.

"I suppose you could call it that," said David.

"That's not nice," said Caroline, "to describe it as bribery."

By this time I had seated myself and begun the assault on the unsuspecting piece of pumpkin cake. Contrary to my mother's instructions, I tried to talk and eat at the same time, so what came out sounded like a wounded cat moaning. "How woo oo deshibe it?"

Renee managed to decipher it anyway and replied, "I called it bait."

For some reason, nearly everyone in the café found that remark irresistibly humorous. I just nodded and kept focused on my cake and cider. When I finished, I said, "OK, I took the bait, and thank you, by the way. So what is the trap?"

"I've been thinking about the Christianity stuff ever since the last time we were here," David said. "And you got me curious with your last remark."

I searched the 64K or so of RAM that serves as my memory and came up with nothing. "Help me out here," I said. "It's been several weeks. I don't remember that last remark."

"You said that despite the heart transplant we get when we become Christians, death still comes to us," Renee said.

"Oh, right," I said, my memory chips warming up. "Well, that's true isn't it?"

"That was OK," said David, "until you added those last three little words."

"Three little words?" I said, "Like the three little words every husband should say to his wife every day?"

"No, not those—" David began, but Renee interrupted him.

"Let the man talk," she said. Then, to me, "Tell my fiancé what three little words a man should say every day to his wife."

"Oh, that's easy. 'I was wrong,' " I said.

Renee looked puzzled, "Wrong about what?"

"It doesn't matter," I said. "It's just wise for a man to get in the habit of saying 'I was wrong' to his wife."

"What if he's not wrong?" asked David.

"Has nothing to do with it," I said.

"OK, guys, very funny," said Renee. "Can we get back to the subject?"

"You were the one who said 'Let the man talk,' " David protested. We both looked with abject innocence at Renee.

She fixed me with a look that teachers reserve for errant schoolboys, and in a tone appropriate to her gaze she said, "Last time you said that death still comes to Christians *for a while.*' " She paused and renewed the power of her gaze. "I'd like an explanation," said Renee. "*We* would like an explanation."

"Oh, that," I said. "Now I remember."

"Well, we've been thinking a lot about it," said Renee. "Doesn't the Bible promise eternal life to Jesus' followers?"

"Yes," I agreed, "but don't Christians still die?" They nodded. "And beyond that, despite that heart transplant, Christians still struggle with sin and still fail to do the right thing?

"Speaking of failure reminds me of something important," I said.

"Jim and Christmas?" several asked at once.

"I've arranged with Rose and Erica to have the café open Christmas Eve. Jim said that's the most important time for him. Growing up, that's when his family opened gifts," I explained. "He has other plans Christmas Day, so that worked best for him."

"I thought you were going to be somewhere else," David said.

"I wasn't planning to come to town that day," I admitted, "and neither was Erica. But we each arranged to bring some family with us here that night, and Rose—against her better judgment, and with the strict guarantee that Erica would be in charge—said we could run the café for that one evening."

"I'm glad," said Renee. "Jim's such a nice guy."

"Yes. We settled it all in time to tell his mother before she died," I said. "I visited her, with Jim, several times before the end. It seemed to please her that someone would be there for Jim."

"How's he doing with that?" asked Caroline.

"He's OK, I guess," said David. "A hospice worker visited Jim and his mother for the last couple of months. Made things easier for both of them, I think."

"And he's getting grief counseling," said Renee.

"But that brings us back to the problem," said David. "Jim's mother still died. Christian or not, we all die. So, what good is Christianity?"

"In one way, it's a lot like hospice," I said. "Ernest Hemingway said 'Every true story ends in death.' "

"You mentioned that once before," said Mark.

"Well, on this earth, it's true," I said. "Every year, millions of people come to the end of their story, and it always ends as Hemingway predicted."

"Hospice doesn't change that," said David.

"No," I agreed, "but it can help people fill the last chapters of their lives with meaning."

. ☕ .

On this earth, at best, we all live in hospice. From the first breath, we begin to form attachments with individuals whom we will watch weaken and die. Or they will watch us. The libraries of our memory fill up with biographies ending at all stages of development but all ending in silence.

We perceive the sweetness of life and cling to existence in spite of suffering, grief, and discouragement. The same consciousness that allows us to enjoy the exhilaration of existence also confronts us with the reality that we must relinquish both existence and consciousness.

We barely reach maturity and experience our full physical and mental powers before they begin to wane. When death tarries, the passing years loosen our grip on life as aging robs us of vitality and ability. Even as our powers decline, we remain painfully aware of our losses. Worse, the longer we live, the more we witness the physical and mental decline and death of others close to us.

Life is sweet, but the longer we live, the more suffering we experience, both personally and vicariously. The Bible writers also address this sad dilemma of existence. "The length of our days is seventy years—or eighty, if we have the strength; yet their span is but trouble and sorrow."

" 'Man born of woman is of few days and full of trouble. He springs up like a flower and withers away; like a fleeting shadow, he does not endure.' "

. ☕ .

"I don't like talking about this," said Caroline.

"It makes me angry," said David.

"Of course," I said. "None of us likes it, and it makes all of us angry if we let it. The poet Dylan Thomas urged us not to 'Go gentle into that good night,' and to 'Rage, rage, against the dying of the light.' Singer Peggy Lee plaintively asked 'Is that all there is?' While an old spiritual inquires, 'And Am I Born to Die?'

"And even in the Bible, the Preacher—*Ecclesiastes* means Preacher—complained: 'And I declared that the dead, who had already died, are happier than the living, who are still alive.' Repeatedly, the Preacher tells us that life is 'emptiness.' Reason enough to rage."

"Yeah, we got it," said David, "death's a real problem. But what answer does Christianity have?"

"There is one answer," I said, "in two parts."

"Is this a riddle," said Caroline, "because I'm too tired for a riddle."

"According to Christianity, God's answer to all these problems—to sin, evil, and especially to death, is Jesus," I said. "And the two parts are the two times Jesus comes to earth to deal with sin."

· ☕ ·

God responded to this desperate situation by sending His Son. John records Jesus' ringing declaration of hope, " 'I am the resurrection and the life. He who believes in me will live, even though he dies.' "

The light that shines from Christ's empty tomb brightens our whole lives, especially the final hours. No matter how difficult our days, how great our suffering, how short the span of our lives, we can face death with hope. Our personal story may conclude with death, but the resurrection offers the promise of an epilogue, of pages yet to be added and filled. Because of the resurrection, "Never again will death have the last word."

· ☕ ·

"You still haven't answered the question, as I see it," said Mark. "The resurrection offers hope, but death still stalks the land. If God can loosen death's grip, why doesn't He eliminate it altogether?"

"God has a plan to do just that," I said. "Even before the Resurrection, before the Crucifixion, Christ assured the disciples that He would not leave the conquest of death half done. He promised to return. He's coming back to finish off sin and death."

"What's the significance of the Second Coming versus the First?" asked Mark, ever analytical.

"When He came the first time, Christ *defeated* death, when He comes the second time, He will *destroy* death!" I said. "The first time He *gave hope* to the suffering and dying; the second time He will *eliminate* suffering and death. The first time, Christ came to share *our suffering and even death*; the second time He will come so that *we can share His life*!

"You'll especially appreciate this, Mark," I said. "The Bible tells us the wages of sin is death.

"On the cross, Jesus accepted those wages for all who trust in Him. But those who reject Him must receive payment. Satan has been piling up 'earnings' a long time in God's ledger."

"So, when He returns, Jesus will settle all the accounts?" asked Mark.

"That's right. As I said, on the cross, Jesus settled the account for all those who accept Him, but those who insist on getting what they deserve will receive that final, fearful payment," I said. "And then, with all accounts settled, death itself will be destroyed. As the Bible tells us, 'The last enemy to be destroyed is death.'

"Those who trusted in Christ will be resurrected. And this time, there will be, as the Bible says, 'No more death, neither sorrow, nor crying, neither shall there be any more pain: for the former things are passed away.'

"No more earth-as-hospice. No more waiting for death. No more grieving for lost loved ones. No more goodbyes."

"Ooooh," said Caroline, "I can't wait for that to happen."

"That's what everyone waits for," I said.

"How long will it be?" asked David. "How long do we have to wait?"

"For a while," I said.

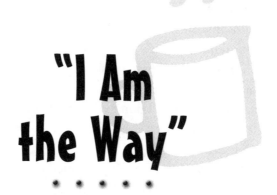

"I Am the Way"

• • • • •

I really like the café," David said, "but I've pretty much decided that Christianity isn't for me."

Renee looked devastated. "Are you sure?"

"Don't try to talk me out of it," David warned her.

"Talk you out of it?" I said. "Not for a moment. God Himself safeguards your choice. I couldn't 'talk you out of it' if I wanted to."

David frowned. "I thought that's what this place was all about. Talking people into becoming Christians?"

"No, David," I said. "Our name says it all: Grounds for Belief exists to help those who want to understand the Christian faith better."

"So, all these games, and the food, that's just a come-on?" asked David.

"David! What's got into you? I've never heard you talk like this," said Renee.

"It's all right," I said. "Honest questions are always welcome here. No," I said, turning to David, "the games and the food aren't a come-on, as you call it. Those things are here because they are a part of the Christian life we have chosen."

"Food and fun games are part of the Christian life?" David asked, obviously puzzled. "I thought Christianity was about punishing yourself and doing without—sacrifice, that sort of thing."

"Oh, there will be sacrifices enough for anyone who chooses to be a

Christian. The first one, though, is choosing to follow Jesus," I said. "That can be quite frightening."

"Who said anything about being afraid?" David asked, a little too quickly. Behind him, Renee's eyes grew wide with recognition. "Besides, what do you mean by 'following Jesus'?"

"Did you know I'm afraid of heights?" I asked. David seemed a little confused by the question. "I don't even like being this tall," I said, eliciting a giggle from Caroline. "I get a nosebleed on a stepladder," I said, arching my eyebrows.

"I'm serious," said David, clearly irritated.

"Oh, I'm serious too," I said. "So seriously afraid of heights that, years ago, I could think of only one thing to do."

"OK, I give," said David. "What did you do?"

"I took a rock-climbing course to confront my fear of heights head-on. The third day of class . . ."

· ☕ ·

I stood poised at the edge of the precipice, nothing but very thin air between me and the ground eighty feet below. "Now lean back over the edge," the instructor told me. "Go ahead, sit down," he urged as I gingerly lowered the sitting portion of my anatomy over the cliff. This day of my rock-climbing class was dedicated to rappelling—gliding gracefully down the cliff. In theory. As I lowered myself over the abyss, I contemplated that theory in some detail.

The friction of the rope as it wound its way around my body and through the sturdy steel carabiners would slow my descent. By guiding the rope around more or less of my body, I could increase or decrease the total friction, which would produce a corresponding decrease or increase in the rate of descent. As I peered over the edge, that knowledge did not quiet my increasingly agitated solar plexus. I was frightened.

Like many people, I learn more easily by doing rather than reading or hearing. All the more when what I'm learning involves significant personal risk. My unfortunate encounters with the law of gravity told me that a fall of eighty feet qualified as a significant risk. But when I watched another person, no more immune to gravity than myself, show me how, it gave me the courage to try. The instructor's example and encouragement helped me get over the edge and down that rope. "You can do it," he called. "Just do what you saw me do."

Each day of the class, our teacher had demonstrated that day's technique, and then coached us in turn as we did our best to duplicate his actions. Our confidence grew daily as we saw our teacher perform that day's assigned tasks. Although I never became a great mountain climber, that class taught me a lot.

. ☕ .

"Every one of you," I said, looking around, "is facing, one way or another, the same type of predicament that I faced on that cliff years ago. You face a future you cannot avoid, you're uncertain about your fate, and yet you are confronting a number of choices that will alter your life permanently."

"Like?" David asked.

"You're young, just beginning to live on your own," I said, "so you face the question of how to live your life to the full. That includes a whole host of other questions, like what faces you at the end of life and, for some of you, right now, the question of what to do with this Person called Jesus.

"All these serious questions loom before you like a precipice," I said. "You feel that once you commit there's no going back, and you worry that on the way down you may discover that the experience doesn't match your expectations. What if you regret the choice after you make it?

"Whether we want to or not, every day we face choices that will change our lives forever. Since we get only one go-around, we desperately want to make the right choices. Isn't that so?" I asked, looking from one sober face to another.

"Philosopher Henry David Thoreau said he did not want to come to the end of life only to discover that he had not really lived. Every one of us," I said, "including older people like me, needs to find the secret to living well each day—so well that, no matter when the end of life comes, no matter the painful experiences along the way, we can know in our inmost being that we have lived, and lived well.

"But you've got a problem unique to your age," I said. "And there's nothing anyone can do about it."

"What kind of problem?" asked David, no longer defensive.

"Up to now, most of you have spent your whole lives doing what others have told you to do," I said, "and the truth is that you're tired of it. Am I wrong?" No one disagreed.

"Your lives seem filled with *rules* and not with *living*. You're surrounded by people—parents, teachers, friends—all trying to tell you the right thing to do. Hmm?" I looked around and saw assent. "And it has always been so. Whether from Confucius or Socrates or Buddha, human beings have never lacked for good advice about how to live.

"Well, I faced that same precipice all those years ago, about how to live my life. I was young, had a good job and a beautiful wife. But I wasn't happy."

"What did you do?" said David, earnestness in his voice and on his face. He looked at me as if only the two of us existed. Behind him, a tear traced its way down Renee's cheek.

I looked back at David with the same intense focus, my voice low. "I realized something had to change. I had been raised in a religious home, but like many others, I found all the rules tiring and irrelevant to my real life."

I looked from side to side, as if to assure him that no one else could hear, while actually everyone was leaning in, my voice barely above a whisper. "Not only that, but I didn't much care for the very ones who claimed to live by all the rules."

I sat back, took a deep breath, and resumed a normal tone. "Problem was, like learning to rappel, I needed more than theory; I needed a friend to show me how."

David nodded slowly, and I heard several grunts of assent.

"That's what made Jesus different from all the rest. He didn't say 'Follow the rule book.' No, He said 'Follow Me.' He didn't say 'I know the way'; He said 'I am the Way.' "

"Yes, but what does that mean?" asked David.

Quickly I rose and got a copy of *The Message* from Rose's bookshelf. Paging through as I walked, I found the passage and sat down. "Here's the best description I've found. ' "Are you tired? Worn out? Burned out on religion? Come to me. Get away with me and you'll recover your life. I'll show you how to take a real rest. Walk with me and work with me—watch how I do it. Learn the unforced rhythms of grace. I won't lay anything heavy or ill-fitting on you. Keep company with me and you'll learn to live freely and lightly." '

"And that has made all the difference."

"What has?"

"Once I knew where to look, I found friends who knew Jesus. We share our lives with each other—even good food and fun games . . ." here I winked at David, "as He shares His life with us. Every day we learn more of what it means to live 'freely and lightly.' Each of us has trials and sorrows, but we're learning how to live well through difficult times. We support each other when discouraged and celebrate each other's triumphs."

"I don't know," David said.

"It's not about knowing," I said. "I did learn to rappel that day, but not from studying the theory. I had to take the plunge. The same is true for following Jesus. You'll never know how to do it by studying religion. You can only know if you try it. You might like it."

A Note for the Reader

• • • • •

In the introduction I said everyone's welcome at our café. If you've come this far, I hope you enjoyed the journey, and I hope that you have found at least some of the answers you seek.

As far as David's choice goes, I cannot tell you. Each one who makes the journey must tell his or her own story. And the choice that remains is not about knowing but about taking the plunge, about following Jesus, about becoming—becoming a Christian. Or not. No one can make the choice for David, or for you.

Should you choose to follow Jesus, I say "Welcome, fellow traveler." Don't attempt the journey alone. Find someone who knows Jesus—perhaps the person who recommended this book. Or, if you'd like to meet one of my friends, contact me at pastored@groundsforbelief.com

Don't waste time with those who simply want to talk doctrine. Don't be put off by the phonies and the wannabes. You'll meet them in any group. "Everybody talkin' 'bout heaven ain't goin' there." So look for those who understand what a friendship with Jesus means, who live "freely and lightly," who know "the unforced rhythms of grace." Don't worry. If you seek them, God will send them to you. Spend some time with them. Discover common interests to base a friendship on. Learn to trust. Get a taste of the life. You, too, might like it.

I hope you'll accept the invitation, because God has promised to banish death and remake this old earth. I plan to be there for the Grand

Opening of the New Earth. It literally will be an unending celebration. The most interesting people from all the ages will be there—I understand the apostle John really knows how to tell a funny story. God, the original Inventor of the good time, will be our Host. I hope you'll join us. It won't be the same without you.

If you enjoyed this book, you'll want to read these:

Cleansing Fire, Healing Streams
Kent A. Hansen

There is transforming power in the realization that you are loved unconditionally and eternally. A longing for something more lives in the hearts of men and women who look thoughtfully at the world, who consider their own human condition and limitations.

Kent A. Hansen, husband, father, civic leader, successful and respected attorney, is one of those who has looked thoughtfully, considered his own condition, and been changed by God's grace. "I write my personal experience not to bare my soul, for that alone helps no one," he says. "I am telling you out of my personal knowledge about the cleansing and healing that is possible with Jesus Christ."

The brief and honest chapters in this book will appeal to both men and women. Read them in silence and solitude. Let the underbrush and overgrowth of busyness burn away. Make way for the cleansing springs of grace to flow again through your heart and soul, and share what you discover with others.
Paperback, 288 pages.   0-8163-2179-5   US$16.99

Swimming Against the Current
Chris Blake

Swimming Against the Current contains stories, poems, questions, and observations. You will disagree with some of the many short chapters. Others, you will exult in. Either way, you'll find some new thoughts, and some of them will stick with you.

Author Chris Blake notes, "When Jesus says, as He does often, 'He who has ears, let him hear,' He means *hear what you should.* God exhorts the lazy to "work harder" and the workaholic to "take it easy," and the sluggard relaxes as the frenzied worker increases effort. The question is not, What do I agree with? The question is, What do I need to hear?"

Read these diverse messages and listen for the voice of the Holy Spirit urging you to spiritual growth and practical course corrections in your life.
Paperback, 288 pages.   0-8163-2141-8   US$15.99